111 Things That Help Grieving

Alchemy of the Heart

Love Loss Grief Transformation

Eternal Love

C. Eldon Taylor

111 Things That Help Grieving
Alchemy of the Heart
Love Loss Grief Transformation
Eternal Love

©2016 C. Eldon Taylor

ISBN: 0692707530
ISBN-13: 978-0692707531

LCCN: 2016907549

All rights reserved. No part of this book may be reproduced in any form or by any means, electronic or mechanical, including photocopying, recording, or by any information storage and retrieval system, without written permission except in the case of brief quotations embodied in critical articles and reviews.

This book is intended as a grief/bereavement self help resource and is not intended as a substitute or replacement for the services of medical, mental health, or other helping/healing professionals.

Printed in USA
by CreateSpace

Published by
C. Eldon Taylor
Henrico, Virginia 23228

to
Carol Susan
always forever and beyond

111 Things That Help Grieving

Table of Contents

Introduction   page 1

Section 1: Experience of Grief: Words Concepts Images
1. Hellfires of Grief   7
2. Disbelief   10
3. Raw   12
4. Crying   14
5. Woundedness   17
6. Soft Heart Open Heart Broken Heart   20
7. Disembodied   22
8. Black Lightning   24
9. Life Transforming Moments   26
10. Chakras & Subtle Energy   28
11. Chakra Cords/Chakra Connections   31
12. Chaos of Grief/Stages of Grief   36
13. Reality of My Experience   40
14. Installment Plan Grieving   42
15. Triggers   44
16. Holidays Are Hell   48
17. Regrets and Remorse   50
18. Death As Advisor/Death As Companion   52
19. Widower/Widow   54
20. Complicated Grief   56
21. Sadness and Depression   59

Section 2: Activities/Actions/Doing
22. Honoring The Dead   64
23. Honoring Last Wishes/Last Requests   68
24. Naming Grief/Image of Grief   70
25. Life Review   74

26. Ceremonies	77
27. Moratorium On Holidays	80
28. Maintaining Traditions	82
29. Grief Work	84
30. Memories and Reminisces	87
31. Establishing A Shrine	90
32. Elements At The Shrine	92
33. Flowers At The Shrine	93
34. Lighting Candles	94
35. Burning Incense	95
36. Photographs	96
37. Music	98
38. Memorials	99
39. Wearing Black	102
40. Planting A Tree	104
41. Using Disembodied's Things	106
42. Removing Sick Room Things	108
43. Sharing Stories	109
44. Black Bow Door Decoration	112
45. Journaling	114
46. Dream Journaling	116
47. Poems/Poetry	119
48. Reading Bereavement Books	124
49. Grief Memoirs	127
50. A Meditation To Ease Grief (CD)	132
51. Projects	134

Section 3: Healing

52. Healing	137
53. Golden Dreams	140
54. Messages	142
55. Inspirations	145
56. Making Room	148
57. Forgiveness	150

58. Within My Limitations	152
59. Eyes of Love/Eyes of Loss	154
60. Possession In Great Measure	156
61. Kindness	158
62. Courage To Grieve	161
63. Animal Companion	164
64. Compassion	166
65. Enough	168
66. Achieving Balance	170
67. Quintessence, Sharing (Alchemy)	172
68. Soulmates Spiritmates	175
69. Soulmates Guardian Angels	180
70. Soror Mystica (Alchemy)	182
71. Talking With My Spirit Companion	186
72. Support Of Family and Friends	188
73. Residual Energy	190
74. Grief Journey/Healing Journey	192
75. Spirit Warrior	195
76. Basic Bodily Functions	198
77. Energy Work/Energy Healing	200
78. Grief Counseling	202
79. Massage Therapy	204
80. Acupuncture	205
81. Grief and Disease	206
82. Gratitude	209

Section 4: Book Resources

83. A Time To Grieve	213
84. How To Heal A Grieving Heart	215
85. Transcending Loss	217
86. The Way Men Heal	219
87. Swallowed By A Snake	221
88. Being With Dying	223
89. Dion Fortune's Book Of The Dead	226

90. On Grief And Grieving	229
91. On Dreams And Death	233
92. Grief Dreams	237
93. The Five Ways We Grieve	239
94. I Wasn't Ready To Say Goodbye	241
95. Journey of Souls	243
95. Healing A Spouse's Grieving Heart	245
97. Shaman, Healer, Sage	247
98. A Shaman's Miraculous Tools	249
99. One Spirit Medicine	250
100. The Emerald Tablet	251

Section 5: Alchemy Of The Heart

101. Alchemical Concepts & Images	255
102. Alchemical Processes & Operations	257
103. Alchemy of Love/Alchemy of Loss	260
104. Calcination (fire)	263
105. Dissolution (water)	266
106. Separation (air)	269
107. Conjunction (earth)	271
108. Fermentation	274
109. Distillation	276
110. Coagulation	279
111. Transformation/Transmutation	281

Index	283
Acknowledgements	288
Copyright Acknowledgements/Permissions	290
Author	295
Other Works By The Author	296

111 Things That Help Grieving

Introduction

The loss of a loved one is one of the most intense and traumatic experiences of an embodied life time. Depending on the nature of the relationship and energy connections, the loss may be THE most intense and traumatic experience of an embodied lifetime.

On October 31, 2011 my beloved soulmate, Carol Susan, disembodied as her beautiful radiant spirit left her physical body to return to our spirit realm home. The disembodiment of my soulmate has been THE most intense and traumatic experience of my embodied life. I have experienced the hellfires of grief, black nights of the soul, a broken heart, and my embodied soul's lament. The image is of being repeatedly struck by invisible black lightning during a raging storm that has no end.

The work of grief is grieving. This may seem self evident; however, in a culture that abhors dying, death, grief, and grieving; the work of grieving is encouraged to remain underground – to be experienced in private or better still forgotten. **111 Things That Help Grieving** offers suggestions and recommendations to honor the disembodied (usually called "the dead") and to honor the embodied (usually called "the living"). Achieving balance between honoring the disembodied and honoring the embodied is complex work and a major focus of many of the world's wisdom traditions.

The work of grief is complicated by seeing primarily through eyes of loss. Recovery of seeing with eyes of love brings healing energy essential for the work of grieving. The transformation is a slow and painful process as eyes of loss often prevail. A major focus of **111 Things That Help Grieving** is to slowly and with great effort restore the balance between loss and love so that love continues to flow between the two souls – one embodied – one disembodied.

A heart broken by loss is also an open heart that may enable the embodied to receive the healing energy of love from the disembodied. I experience golden dreams where I visit the spirit realm and my beloved as well as experiencing subtle messages and inspirations. Golden dreams, messages, and inspirations are blessings beyond measure as they bring the healing energy of the spirit realm and provide the experience of ongoing love.

111 Things That Help Grieving is organized in five sections. The first section presents the experience of grief in words, concepts, and images to lick the woundedness of loss with healing energy.

The second section consists of actions – things to do – activities. A major emphasis is establishing sacred space and ceremonies that honor the disembodied and embodied. Ceremonies and other actions provide comfort, solace, and healing energy.

Section three focuses on healing in concentrated form. Healing is an ongoing process as the woundedness of loss is a lifelong experience. The loss of a loved one is a raw, black, heavy, and painful experience. After loss we will never be the same as before nor should we expect to be. Healing from loss is a complex process described in energy terms rather than physical woundedness.

Section four recommends the eighteen books that have provided the most benefit of the many death, dying, grief, grieving, and bereavement books I have read. Each book is briefly described with a few brief quotations included to enable sampling the book's voice.

Section five, Alchemy of the Heart, uses the images, language, and processes of alchemy in a feeble attempt to comprehend the mysteries of **love** – the radiant gold of abundance in great measure and **loss** – the black lead of abundance in great measure with the abundance being **grief** and the experience of the hellfires of grief and black nights of the soul. The mysteries of **transformation** are explored using alchemical processes to describe a small golden flame in the midst of the black fires of grief. One of the final mysteries hidden within the hellfires of grief is **eternal love** – abundance beyond measure. Alchemy of the heart describes love loss grief transformation eternal love swirling in the heart of hearts of the embodied soul whose loved one has disembodied.

I hope the words, concepts, images, and activities presented in **111 Things That Help Grieving** help you lick the woundedness of your loss, assist you in the discovery of healing energy, and provide a measure of comfort, solace, and the transformative golden energy of eternal love. May you be blessed beyond measure with golden dreams and eternal love.

C. Eldon Taylor
May 8, 2016

Section One

Experience of Grief
Words Concepts Images

Words are inadequate to fully describe the experience of the loss of a loved one. Words attempt to translate soul's tears and describe the chaos within one's heart of hearts that results after the disembodiment of a loved one. Even within their limitations, words have power. Words are offered to honor the disembodied and to offer comfort, solace, and healing to the embodied. May the words of **111 Things That Help Grieving** provide you with ways to honor your loved one, assist you in finding a measure of balance between loss and love, and to experience the healing energy of ongoing eternal love. Love does not die with the disembodiment of your loved one, love becomes more subtle. May you be blessed beyond measure with the experience of eternal love. If your grief is too dark, raw, and heavy to fully experience the love flowing between the physical and spirit realms, I hope the words of **111 Things That Help Grieving** assist you in strengthening your connection so you fully experience eternal love.

111 Things That Help Grieving

"The death of a beloved is an amputation…"

Madeleine L'Engle

111 Things That Help Grieving: **#1**

Hellfires of Grief

"'He extinguishes the fire in its own inner measure.'…the fire has to burn the fire, one just has to burn in the emotion till the fire dies down and becomes balanced. That is something which unfortunately cannot be evaded. The burning of the fire, of the emotion, cannot not be tricked out of one's system; there is no recipe for getting rid of it, it has to be endured. The fire has to burn until the last unclean element has been consumed, which is what all alchemical texts say in different variations, and we have not found any other way either. It cannot be hindered but only suffered till what is mortal or corruptible, or as our text says so beautifully, till the corruptible humidity, the unconsciousness, has been burnt up. That is the meaning, it is the acceptance of suffering. …Sitting in Hell and roasting there is what brings forth the philosopher's stone; as it is said here, the fire is extinguished with its own inner measure."*
Marie-Louise von Franz

There are different types of fire. Common physical realm fire is only one type. Common fire needs no description nor is it the type of fire we experience in the hellfires of grief. There are emotional fires - fires in the belly, heart fires, and mental fires to name just a few major fires. These fires are not like common physical realm fire which consumes and destroys what it burns. The fires in the belly, heart, and mind are subtle fires burning with intensity yet not destroying. Hot with no heat, burning with no destruction, and often invisible to the physical senses. In times of love the fires are bright yet invisible to most. Heart fires golden with love. The subtle fires are intensified by the connections between people. The more connections the more intense the fire. With loss the fire transforms into the hellfires of grief. From gold the fire turns black burning with great intensity. The hellfires of grief transform the golden rainbow fires of love into darkness, chaos, and the underworld of loss. The night-sea journey begins and blackness prevails.

What the hellfires of grief are consuming as fuel are the regrets, remorse, doubts, errors of omission, and errors of commission – all of the flaws of one's nature. All of the unrefined thoughts, trauma of loss, experience of rejection although unintended by the disembodied loved one, the empty space as all of the connections of the lower chakras are now severed, flailing, losing energy, and looking hopelessly for their counterpart in the physical realm.

With improved vision as a result of active grieving, grief work, golden dreams, inspirations, and other subtle messages; the hellfires of grief may not actually burn any less intensely; however, vision is expanded beyond the black fire. Golden dreams and other experiences lead to the eventual discovery that surrounding the black hellfires of grief are golden, silver, and rainbow fires. It appears the black hellfires of grief are embraced by the gold, silver, and rainbow fires of love. Perhaps the hellfires of grief burn a little less intensely having burned off enough impurities to allow an expanded vision to transcend the black hellfires of grief, at least for a while. The expanded reality of experience provides the healing energy of ongoing love surrounding the heart and holding it together with the healing energy of love.

*Marie-Louise von Franz. **Alchemy: An Introduction to the Symbolism and the Psychology.** 1980, pages 252 and 254.

111 Things That Help Grieving: #2

Disbelief

I experience attacks of disbelief that seem beyond simple denial. I look at photographs and then remember, really remember, she is no longer embodied. Of course I know at the level of my head that she has been disembodied for over four years. As I write this, I am sitting beside her ashes in her black marble urn at her shrine. Still there are moments when I experience intense disbelief. My experience of disbelief seems very primitive and results in intense sadness and despair. I cannot resist wondering why – why my beloved got sick and disembodied at only 57 years old. I have no better answers now than I did years ago. I invent answers and reject them all. Below the disbelief is the reality of my experience of loss, missing, and despair. Even with the experience of golden dreams and other messages, I continue to experience attacks of disbelief that she is no longer embodied. The attacks of disbelief cause me to stop, remember, and begin the questions over again. Before the questions, I attempt to deny saying "NO!" then the questions "WHY?" followed by the only response that seems authentic at the time "DAMN!"

I would like to be able to say that with each episode I seem a bit less sad and a bit less despairing; however, that is not the reality of my experience. I am shocked with each episode of disbelief as if I am suddenly aware she has really disembodied. I would like to be able to say that with each episode of disbelief I perceive myself to be dropping ever lower in the dragon named grief while the dragon named grief drops ever lower within me. I cannot state that either except at an intellectual fantasy level. The reality of my experience is that I suddenly remember, **really remember**, and **know** she has disembodied abandoning her physical body. The reality of my experience is that she is no longer of the physical realm. Her disembodiment seems such a waste, as well as a cruel and random act of stupidity. During my attacks of disbelief, I rail at death who is not my advisor but a blood thirsty, sharp toothed old hag who has lost any semblance of sense or reason. I also rail against the fates who I accuse of taking a nap or not paying proper attention to their tasks. None of my ruminations and railings about the ugly reality of death lessens my shock and disbelief when I am suddenly freshly struck by the awful awareness that she is gone from the physical realm.

I cannot offer suggestions about improving this aspect of grieving and disbelief. I share the experience of ongoing episodes of intense and painful disbelief in order to acknowledge the experience.

111 Things That Help Grieving: #3

Raw

Not long after the disembodiment of my beloved, a hospice grief counselor called to check on me. While we talked about any number of things, the comment she made about how raw I was likely feeling provided me with an excellent one word description of my emotional condition. I adopted the concept of rawness and discovered when I told others about my rawness, the word conveyed a powerful image. Having a summary word for my emotional experience of loss and grief was strangely comforting. My rawness was not diminished by naming it but the concept of rawness described the edges of my pain and suffering and communicated it to others. I soon added the words "dark" and "heavy" to the concept of rawness. Dark was more often black and heavy often included numb.

With the loss of my loved one I suffered an intense, severe wound. While the woundedness may not be visible, the wound can be life threatening. Words have power. The image I have is that of me licking my woundedness with words. The licking may help more than you know in your head. Just as the wound may not show, subtle healing may not be visible. Much licking and many words are necessary. Years and years of licking and years and years of words.

While the summary words, "raw", "dark", and "heavy", do not significantly diminish the pain and suffering of loss; the words had a calming effect on the swirling chaos experienced after the loss of my loved one. The words summarized the condition of my heart of hearts and embodied soul. My energy systems – raw and bleeding; my heart broken in two; my embodied soul separated from the embodied soul of my companion - raw, dark, and heavy at being left behind.

Note: For a better understanding of the concept of rawness and woundedness when looking at the impact of loss and grief on energy systems, specifically the concept of chakra connections see Chakra Cords/Chakra Connections, #11, page 31.

111 Things That Help Grieving: **#4**

Crying

Crying is not condoned and often punished by ridicule or less subtle methods. Big boys don't cry. Men don't cry. Big girls do not cry either. Cry Baby. Grin and bear it. Suck it up. Tough it out. Keep a stiff upper lip. Take it like a man. Don't be a crybaby. Push through it. Get a hold of yourself. Get on with your life. I am sure you can add many more.

Crying is a release of control. A letting go of the belief of being in charge when the heart overwhelms the head with emotion. When experiencing the mysteries of life and death, made most intense with the loss of a loved one, being overwhelmed and "reduced to tears" is the reality of one's experience. Sometimes a "good cry" is the only activity that helps. Even a "good cry" does not recover the loss but tears release some of the energy of grief when all else fails. Tears are one of the languages of the soul. Tears are the soul's words.

Crying in public is taboo. Shame on you! Crying in private may seem wrong as well. People are conditioned not to show weakness. Crying as weakness. Crying may be increasingly difficult to experience. So if you have difficultly crying give yourself permission to cry. Crying is sometimes the only response to catastrophic loss. It has been said that eyes are the window to the soul. Tears are the soul's words when all other words are inadequate.

Since crying in public is taboo, crying may go underground. The release of tears by crying is a cleansing action. Holding on to tears by not releasing them causes tears to be stored in the physical body (as well as several levels of subtle energy bodies). Hording tears does not allow for a cleansing release and creates an environment that becomes increasingly ripe for unshed tears to be converted into less desirable modes of expression.

Tears acknowledge that we are powerless in the face of the mysteries of life and death. The disembodiment of your loved one is the single most traumatic experience of a lifetime. Hopefully you experience the good fortune of being unable to contain your tears. Blessed that you are unable to repress or suppress your anguish, grief, and tears. While you may be able to wear and maintain your public face in public, you will have been blessed if you can find a sacred space where you can release your tears without negative reactions of others and especially without your own negative appraisal of your need to release your pent up tears. In our culture it is more acceptable to express anger than sadness, heartbreak, and grief with tears.

Before Carol Susan disembodied, I would cry in the shower as crying in her presence made her cry and amplified her pain. Sometimes I could not contain the tears but often I took to crying in the shower. Carol Susan would ask me if I was crying in the shower and I would tell her "no, of course not." She knew I was crying in the shower. I still cry in the shower remembering her last months, weeks, days. Our last times embodied together. I cry at her shrine. I cry when ever and where ever I am in the house we picked out and fixed up together. Sometimes I cry in the car especially when going by places we visited when both embodied. Not long after Carol Susan disembodied after one of my crying times, I told her I was making up for holding back my tears. I could not hold back my tears nor did I want to. I know she was pleased.

I hope you have a sacred space were you can take off your public face and give yourself permission to have a "good cry." For some people their souls grant permission to cry even if they do not want to shed tears. The soul knows the wisdom of releasing tears even if the head is resistant. If you are unable to cry consider some releasing activities. Triggers to assist you in letting go in a safe private space.

111 Things That Help Grieving: **#5**

Woundedness

"The death of a beloved is an amputation…"*
                                    Madeleine L'Engle

In the introduction to C.S. Lewis' **A Grief Observed**, Madeleine L'Engle describes the disembodiment of her beloved husband as "an amputation."

"One of the most painful experiences in life is to lose a loved one through abandonment, divorce, or death. The cords usually get badly damaged in these experiences. I have seen all the chakras on the front of the body torn open, with the cords floating out in space, after such trauma. The personal experience of such a trauma is described as the feeling of being torn apart, or as if their better half is missing. Many people become disoriented and don't know what to do with themselves."**
                                    Barbara Ann Brennan

Barbara Ann Brennan is writing about the experience of the loss of a loved one using the language of subtle energy centers (chakras) and the subtle energy connections to ones beloved (chakra cords) which she describes a form of energy amputation.

While these are subtle body and subtle energy amputations, the experience is anything but subtle. In describing the changes to chakras and energy bodies at death Barbara Ann Brennan indicates "...the lower three bodies were breaking up..." (etheric, emotional, mental) "The lower three chakras were also breaking up..." (base/root, sacral, solar plexus)***

The lower energy bodies and lower chakras break up as the individual disembodies and their soul – their life force abandons their physical body. The experience for those left behind is felt at multiple levels of physical and subtle energy bodies. The chakra cords or connections are suddenly severed creating an energy amputation in which the chakra cords of the embodied person hemorrhage energy and flail about seeking to reconnect with their counter parts. The subtle energy woundedness is often described as having a broken heart with the intense physical experiences of pain and suffering. I describe the experiences as being in the hellfires of grief, swallowed by the dragon named grief, swallowing the dragon named grief, and being struck by invisible black lightning. The woundedness is not only to the subtle energy centers and energy bodies, but the physical body also experiences intense mental, emotional and physical pain. The embodied soul has lost its connection to its soulmate in the physical realm; therefore, the embodied soul is also wounded and experiences intense pain.

The descriptions of energy bodies and energy, centers and their reactions to the loss of ones beloved provided by Barbara Ann Brennan in her two books about energy healing have provided me with words with which to lick my woundedness and concepts to promote regaining my balance, as well as the promise of healing, even if slow and painful. Many of the **111 Things That Help Grieving** are focused on ministering to and healing my and other's woundedness. My journaling and poems are ways of licking my woundedness with words. The alchemical concepts, images, and processes provide both a description of the condition of woundedness as well as ways to potential healing.

For expanded information about chakras and chakra cords/chakra connections see Things That Help Grieving #10 (page 28) and #11 (page 31). For additional information about alchemy of the heart see Things That Help Grieving #101 - #111 (pages 255-281).

*Madeleine L'Engle, Introduction to C.S. Lewis, **A Grief Observed**, Harper Collins, 1961, page xii.

Barbara Ann Brennan, **Light Emerging: The Journey of Personal Healing, Bantam Books, 1993, page 186.

***Barbara Ann Brennan, **Hands of Light: A Guide to Healing Through the Human Energy Field**, Bantam Books, 1988, page 68.

111 Things That Help Grieving: **#6**

Soft Heart, Open Heart, Broken Heart

The loss of a loved one is a heart breaking experience. With the loss of my soulmate I experienced my heart breaking over and over. I remember wondering in a moment of irrational rationality how many pieces my heart could break into before disappearing all together. Then my heart would sort of mend back together, raw and painful, cobbled together, and hanging on by a thread. Of course, I am not referring to the heart of my physical body, the one that pumps my blood about. I am referring to my emotional energy heart – the heart of my hearts – home of my embodied soul and portal to the spirit realm.

Many wisdom traditions recommend and teach practices to cultivate a soft and open heart as a key component in developing compassion, empathy, and forgiveness. To have a soft and open heart is to be more aware of the experience of the pain and suffering of yourself and others as well as being more open to experiencing the power and wonder of love. Maintaining a soft and open heart is considered one of the attributes of a spirit warrior.

With the loss of your loved one you will experience a soft and open heart because it has been broken by the loss. A broken heart is an open heart and a soft heart even though raw and anguished. Even if your have been thick skinned, tough, and hard-hearted your loss may result in your being dropped into the experience of your heart's center – like it or not. So if you are shocked to find yourself in the unfamiliar terrain of your heart of hearts, you are experiencing a blessing even if it does not feel like one. For me the feeling has been what I call the hellfires of grief. The more intense your connection to your disembodied loved one the more intense your grief and the more raw and heartbroken your experience.

In many "modern" cultures having a soft and open heart is considered a liability. Statements like "soft touch," "wears his heart on his sleeve," and others are not offered as compliments. Do not allow yourself to be manipulated by those who wish for you to close and harden your heart. While raw and painful, a soft and open heart allows you to fully experience and express your grief. Even if you have always had a soft and open heart the loss of your loved one will most likely result in the discovery that your heart of hearts is much bigger than you could have ever imagined. Your soft and open heart will allow you to become more connected to your embodied soul and to your loved ones in the spirit realm.

111 Things That Help Grieving: **#7**

Disembodied

I use the word "disembodied" rather than the word "dead." We are embodied when our souls enter our body and disembodied when our souls leave. The word "death," even the word "death-of-the-body," is not as accurate or as true as the word "disembodied." If you listen to your soul's whispers, your soul speaks of disembodiment rather than death since souls relocate from the physical realm to the spirit realm.

You may be thinking my preference is only semantic word play or massive denial of the finality of death. Ancient wisdom traditions know words have power. The use of the word "disembodied" acknowledges the existence of the spirit realm while the word "dead" focuses on the physical realm and ignores the spirit realm. Many wisdom traditions tell of souls traveling to the other side, crossing over, parting the veil between the physical realm and the spirit realm, and returning with memories of fantastic experiences in journeying to the spirit realm. Some of these visits we remember as powerful dreams and some are remembered as fantasies, reveries, or visions in altered states of awareness.

Use of the term "disembodied" does not lessen the pain of loss for those left behind after the disembodiment of our loved one. We grieve the loss of our physically embodied loved one no matter which words we use. The use of the word "dead" focuses on loss – seeing with eyes of loss while the word "disembodied" focuses on love – seeing with eyes of love. Both are true and part of the reality of our bereavement experience.

The use of the term "disembodied" as a concept reflects an expanded awareness of the existence of the spirit realm that weakens the veil allowing spirit realm phenomena to be experienced in the physical realm. The intense emotions generated by loss experienced as grief and bereavement may shift the center of awareness from the head to the heart. The heart broken open becomes the center of experience overwhelming the often limited vision of the intellect. The soul's heart-home is our heart of hearts which may have been largely ignored prior to our experience of the disembodiment of our loved one. If you are blessed with an open heart and receptive to the whispered wisdom of your soul, you recognize that our loved ones have transcended to a separate reality.

111 Things That Help Grieving: #8

Black Lightning

When my soulmate and I were reunited in this lifetime, the experience was being struck by gold lightning. The intensity is beyond description though the image of being struck by gold lightning hints at the experience. I later came to understand the experience of being struck by gold lightning was reawakening in the golden cocoon surrounding soulmates.

With the disembodiment of my soulmate, I was struck by black lightning. The intensity is beyond description though the image of being struck by black lightning hints at the experience. At first I thought the black lightning had seriously damaged the golden cocoon. I thought the half containing the energy of my beloved was destroyed beyond repair. Over time, I came to realize it was my half of the golden cocoon that was damaged. My focus on my loss prevented me from seeing that the golden cocoon while altered was not damaged beyond repair. The repair required me using different eyes - a different way of seeing – using the vision of my heart or hearts to discover the golden cocoon continues to exist. I was assisted in this discovery by golden dreams, inspirations, and other experiences which reassured me that the golden cocoon continues, more subtle now, and sometimes hidden just beyond my experience of being struck by black lightning.

May the images of being struck by gold lightning and black lightning provide you with another way of seeing your love, loss, and ongoing love. May you be blessed with golden dreams, inspirations, and other messages from your beloved to reassure you that while you experience the loss of your loved one in the physical realm, you also continue to experience ongoing love in the spirit realm. Golden dreams, inspirations, and other messages indicate the barrier or veil between the two realms is at least permeable and for some blessed beyond measure the veil is nonexistent.

111 Things That Help Grieving: **#9**

Life Transforming Moments

Moments can transform your life. A major life transforming moment has the power of lightning. I have experienced two such life transforming moments. The first transformational moment was when my soulmate and I found one another again. The "moment" spanned thirty-four years and many lifetimes. The second transformational moment was the disembodiment of my beloved soulmate when her beautiful radiant spirit returned to our spirit realm home. This second "moment" has spanned four and one half years as of this writing.

The disembodiment of my beloved has resulted in an intense desire to transform the grief and bereavement into an improved experience of life expanded beyond the barriers of physical realm experience. At first eyes of loss prevailed, experiencing the loss of my embodied companion with my broken heart. Slowly eyes of love returned, assisted by golden dreams and other subtle indicators. I became aware that a portion of my embodied soul traveled with my disembodied companion as she transitioned through the gates of death into the spirit realm. This means that I am paradoxically both diminished in the physical realm and enriched beyond measure as I have experienced glimpses of our spirit realm home in golden dreams and in other ways.

The ultimate transformational moments are experienced with the power and intensity of lightning. First was experiencing the golden lightning of rediscovery of the golden cocoon of soulmates in the physical realm. Second was experiencing the black lightning with the disembodiment of my soulmate. The lightning of love is golden, radiant, and breaks open the heart with the experience of abundance in great measure. The lightning of loss is black, raw, intensely heavy, and breaks the heart with the experience of abundance of grief in great measure. Slowly, with much assistance, I have discovered that within and surrounding the black lightning of loss is the golden lightning of eternal love. The black lightning of grief continues; however, now I am able to experience glimpses of the golden energy of eternal love and the experience of abundance beyond measure.

I would like to be able to tell you that my glimpses of the spirit realm, subtle presence of my beloved, and other indicators is enough but I am constantly hoping, wishing, and intending for more. I know my embodied soul has unlimited access to the subtle spirit realm but I am only able to remember glimpses.

111 Things That Help Grieving: **#10**

Chakras and other subtle energy systems

Many wisdom traditions have identified subtle energy bodies and subtle energy systems that coexist with the gross physical body. These subtle energy bodies and subtle energy systems are the focus of many healing traditions.

There are multiple layers of subtle energy bodies which some sensitive individuals are able to "see" or intuit with their metasenses. Our metasenses are able to perceive these subtle energy systems and subtle energy bodies even if the knowing remains below our conscious awareness. We speak of vibrations, colors, and energy levels often unaware of the influence of our metasenses, even denying the existence of our metasenses and subtle energies as we are using the information. Energy healers work with subtle energy bodies and subtle energy systems to assist people in maintaining optimal energy as they influence the health and viability of the physical body and physical energy systems. Subtle energy systems include auras, meridians, chakras, tan-t'iens (dan teins), and others.

While a brief introduction of subtle energy is inadequate to do justice to the complexities of subtle energy systems some information is offered to provide a context for the thing that helps grieving: chakra cords which follows.

In 1919, Sir John George Woodroffe, writing as Arthur Avalon, introduced the Eastern concept of chakras to the West in his book **The Serpent Power**. Chakras are subtle energy centers often described as whirling circles or wheels. The major chakras are located along the physical spine from the base or root chakra to the crown chakra just above the physical head. Chakras are associated with both specific physical and subtle organ systems. For individuals who can "see" chakras they are described as having distinctive colors, vibrations, rates of spin, as well a direction of spin. Energy healers and many physical and meditational practices focus on clearing, cleaning, charging, and maintaining healthy chakras as well as other subtle energy systems. While many references describe seven major chakras, others identify additional chakras including at least several above the crown chakra that connect each person to the subtle spirit realm. It is tempting to call these higher chakras celestial chakras or spirit realm energy systems.

Chakras and other subtle energy systems, subtle energy bodies, and subtle energy healing traditions can offer improved understanding of the complexities of grief, grieving, and healing. The concept of severed and flailing chakra cords of the lower chakras that had been connected to the corresponding chakras of my beloved before her disembodiment provided a very powerful energy explanation for the devastating experience of being severed from my embodied love one while the connections of higher chakras remain. (Barbara Ann Brennan, **Hands of Light**) Subtle energy systems, specifically chakra connections, have provided the best understanding of the paradox of my intense loss and longing coexisting with my experience of the ongoing intense connection to my beloved. Eyes of loss focus on severed physical realm connections while eyes of love focus on higher level subtle energy connections.

Selected resources for additional information include:

Alberto Villoldo. **Shaman, Healer, Sage: How To Heal Yourself and Others With the Energy Medicine of the Americas**. 2000

Donna Eden. **Energy Medicine**. 1998

Barbara Ann Brennan. **Light Emerging: The Journey of Personal Healing**. 1993

Barbara Ann Brennan. **Hands of Light: A Guide to Healing Through the Human Energy Field**. 1987

Maureen Lockhart. **The Subtle Energy Body: The Complete Guide**. 2010.

See the thing that helps grieving: **chakra cords (#11)** which follows for an application the concepts and images of subtle energy systems to the experience of loss and grieving.

111 Things That Help Grieving: **#11**

Chakra Cords/Chakra Connections

Chakra cords: "Whenever a person creates a relationship with another human being, cords grow between the two 3A chakras**.** (solar plexus) The stronger the connection between the two people, the stronger and greater in number these cords will be. In cases where a relationship is ending, the cords are slowly disconnected. Cords develop between other chakras of people in relationships also……through this center, (heart chakra) we connect cords to heart centers of those with whom we have a love relationship…. You probably heard the term 'heartstrings,' which refers to these cords."*

Death: "…the lower three bodies were breaking up…" (etheric, emotional, mental) "The lower three chakras were also breaking up…" (base/root, sacral, solar plexus)**

Brennan, Barbara Ann

"Since the cords are connected on the fourth level of the field and higher, which exists before and beyond three-dimensional physical space, many cord connections actually occur before life in the physical dimension begins. They continue to exist even after the death of anyone involved. The cords remain connected to the deceased people, who have left their bodies and are in the astral or spiritual world. Once they are made, these cord connections never cease. They never dissolve. They are beyond the physical world. At physical death, the auric field of the fourth level and higher doesn't really go through much of a change. It simply isn't connected to a physical body anymore. Therefore, it is not surprising that the cord connections remain after physical death.

…The fuller and stronger the relationship, the fuller and stronger the cords. The more interactions in a relationship, the more cords for that relationship. The more relationships we create the more cords we create.

…In intimate, long-term relationships, we build many cords that connect us through all our chakras. It is in this way we build very deep intimate relationships and remain psychically connected to people no matter where they are on earth, and no matter how much time has elapsed since seeing them.

…One of the most painful experiences in life is to lose a loved one through abandonment, divorce, or death. The cords usually get badly damaged in these experiences. I have seen all the chakras on the front of the body torn open, with the cords floating out in space, after such trauma. The personal experience of such a trauma is described as the feeling of being torn apart, or as if their better half is missing. Many people become disoriented and don't know what to do with themselves." ***

Brennan, Barbara Ann

The concept of chakra cords described by Barbara Ann Brennan in her two excellent books on healing using subtle energy systems provided me with a powerful description of my experience of loss and grief. The energy connections between people, especially ones' beloved companion, preexist the current incarnation and continue once ones' loved one disembodies. The chakra cords of the lower three chakras (root, sacral, and solar plexus) and the three lower energy bodies (etheric, emotional, and mental) become severed during disembodiment. The chakra cords of the embodied one left behind in the physical realm hemorrhage energy as they flail about looking for their counterpart so they can reconnect. The image of flailing chakra cords hemorrhaging energy has provided me a powerful description of my experience during and after the disembodiment of my beloved Carol Susan. The heart chakra is significantly impacted in addition to the lower three more physically oriented chakras. The heart chakra is the bridge between the lower and higher energies of the chakra energy system. In my experience all of the chakras are impacted but the impact is almost total devastation for the lower chakras and less intense for the higher level chakras. The heart chakra in many wisdom traditions is the home of the heart of hearts or embodied soul. The embodied soul experiences both the intense devastation of the lower chakras as well as the continued connections of the higher chakras as well as higher level subtle energy bodies.

At first, my focus was almost entirely on physical realm loss – eyes of loss – the raw, heavy, black burning in the hellfires of grief with my lower chakra cords flailing wildly about hemorrhaging energy. With the experience of golden dreams and other subtle messages, I became more aware of my subtle energy connections to my beloved. The concepts and images provided by Barbara Ann Brennan assisted me in expanding my awareness to know that both of my experiences are part of the reality of my expanded experience across realms. The concept of chakra cords and the severing of some with loss and ongoing connections of others enabled me to encounter the paradox of opposites and know both to be true.

After my experiences of golden dreams and other subtle messages, I would be bathed in the golden aura of eternal love for a time. Then I would experience intense anguish missing my embodied companion. My grief was then compounded by feelings of guilt and shame since after being blessed beyond measure with ongoing golden dreams and eternal love, I would revert to eyes of loss focusing on what was missing rather than what continued. Barbara Ann Brennan's concepts about chakra cords provided me with powerful images that have assisted me in maintain both realities without the additional baggage of guilt and shame.

At four and one half years, my lower level chakra cords are less frantic in their flailing and now ooze energy rather than hemorrhage energy. Some chakra cords may have even retracted at least to some degree. They often become reactivated and much more active before and during special days – anniversaries, birthdays, holidays, and other special days. My improved awareness and understanding of chakra cords and subtle energy has provided me with powerful tools; however, the reality of my experience continues to be the disembodiment of my beloved and the severing of my chakra cords. These concepts and images help a little and my intuition suggests that may be as good as it gets. My intuition also suggests that the more I can look through eyes of love, the closer I will be to manifesting golden dreams while awake.

May the images of chakra cord connections and their severing with the disembodiment of a loved one provide you with improved understanding of the paradox of loss of connections on one level (physical realm) and ongoing eternal connections on the other level (spirit realm).

Should you be interested in additional information about subtle energy systems and energy healing I highly recommend Barbara Ann Brennan's books.

*Brennan, Barbara Ann. **Hands of Light: A Guide to Healing Through the Human Energy Field**. Bantam, Books, 1988, * pages 75-76, ** page 68.

***Brennan, Barbara Ann. **Light Emerging: The Journey of Personal Healing**. Bantam Books, 1993, pages 184 and 186.

111 Things That Help Grieving: **#12**

Chaos of Grief/Stages of Grief

Grieving is a time of chaos. There are no neat and tidy steps or stages in the chaos of grief. Grieving is not linear. Grief does not follow a timeframe or schedule. Grieving is not a pretty spiral – a progression from the hellfires of grief to a mystical experience of illumination after a certain period of time. Grief is not bound by the rules of time, rational logic, or any form of orderly progression or process.

In their book, **On Grief and Grieving**, describing the five stages Elisabeth Kubler-Ross and David Kessler write:

"The stages have evolved since their introduction, and they have been very misunderstood over the past three decades. They were never meant to help tuck messy emotions into neat packages. They are responses to loss that many people have, but there is not a typical response to loss, as there is no typical loss. Our grief is as individual as our lives. The five stages…are a part of the framework that makes up our learning to live with the one we lost. They are tools to help us frame and identify what we may be feeling. But they are not stops on some linear timeline in grief. Not everyone goes through all of them or goes in a prescribed order."*

"People often think of the stages as lasting weeks or months. They forget that the stages are responses to feelings that can last for minutes or hours as we flip in and out of one and then another. We do not enter and leave each individual stage in a linear fashion. We may feel one, then another, and back again to the first one."**

The steps or stages may all appear within moments of one another – one stage one minute then another stage the next. Or two or three or more stages all at once. Grief is chaos – ugly, messy, and the most intense experience of life. The concepts of stages or steps are attempts to provide a roadmap or guidebook to the landscape of loss, grief, and grieving - the landscape of the heart. The problem is the landscape of the heart is not a physical place or location. The realm of the heart is not adequately described by rational logical linear thinking. The realm of the heart is experienced in emotions and soul's tears. Images are already one step removed from the experience and words further abstract the experience as they are two steps removed.

So is there value to steps or stages? Perhaps. Depending on intent. If you encounter someone who is grief adverse, they may use the steps or stages to provide you with a negative appraisal and as weapons to pressure you into getting on with your life. The person may be a healthcare professional, family member, friend, colleague, or near total stranger. Even worse, you may apply the concepts of steps or stages to evaluate yourself negatively.

The concepts of stages or steps can be useful if they provide increased understanding that the reality of your experiences is shared by others in a generic kind of way. Therefore, steps and stages provide consensual validation that your experiences are both similar to and different from others. The use of rigid timelines and the expectation that stages unfold in an orderly fashion is not helpful and adds stress to what is already the most stressful of life's experiences.

It may be more helpful to consider grief and grieving to be a chaotic process. Grieving is different for everyone with some common elements. Grieving is a lifelong process. As grief is not an illness or disease, one does not "recover" from the loss of a loved one. One may, over an undetermined period of time, achieve a measure of balance – transcend the exclusive focus on loss and affirm the presence of eternal love.

In a culture that provides one week bereavement leave for the loss of a spouse (if that) and less for other loved ones and recommends a cornucopia of psychotropic pharmaceuticals after two weeks of bereavement (if not sooner), it should not be a surprise that the full force of the culture mobilizes to encourage you to move on. Climb the steps - press on through the stages as quickly as possible. Better yet, skip them all together and just get over it and get on with your life.

In summary, steps or stages may, in benevolent circumstances, offer a general roadmap to experiences shared in the chaos of grieving. Roadmaps are flat two dimensional general guidelines that often leave out more than they describe. They can still provide a valuable service so long as you do not mistake the roadmap for the road.

Words have power and when they are used to manipulate, they are unhelpful and often harmful instead. When the words are used to describe the language of the heart, they can offer comfort and solace during the chaos of grief. Use steps, stages, or any other roadmap that you find helpful in providing positive energy to your woundedness. Reject efforts to manipulate, force, cajole, or pressuring you into abbreviating your grieving process. Even if it is you who is both the manipulator and manipulatee.

*Elizabeth Kubler-Ross and David Kessler. **On Grief and Grieving: Finding the Meaning of Grief Through the Five Stages of Loss**. Scribner, 2005, *page 7, **page18.

111 Things That Help Grieving: **#13**

Reality Of My Experience

When listening to Belleruth Naparstek's CD: **A Meditation To Ease Grief**, I adopted one of the phrases she uses as one of my own. The phrase is "it is the reality of your experience." I personalized the phrase to "it is the reality of my experience" and later shortened it to "reality of my experience." The phrase has become something akin to a mantra for me as it assists me to recover compassion for myself, extend self-forgiveness and loving kindness towards myself when I become self critical about my coping or experience thoughts or feelings that I judge negatively. Using the phrase "it is the reality of my experience" assists me to acknowledge my experience without becoming caught up in a circular process of monkey-minded ruminations and self criticisms. When I am feeling sad and start to become self critical, I say to myself "it is the reality of my experience" which serves to short circuit my negative self assessment and provides me with permission to feel sad without all the extra baggage. The phrase helps me when missing my embodied loved one, being angry about my circumstances, feeling alone and abandoned, and a host of other thoughts and feelings. The phrase does not work for actions or non-actions such as squandering time. The phrase reminds me to accept the reality of my experience without negative judgment complicating my experience of loss. The phrase functions as a thought stopping device or more accurately as a rumination stopping device which allows me to uncomplicate the reality of my experience. I usually add the phrase I have adopted from Carol Susan that "I am doing the best I can within my limitations."

If you indulge in negative self talk or critical self judgments, you might find the phrase "it is the reality of my experience" helpful. Adding the phrase "I am doing the best I can within my limitations" may also prove helpful. I recommend Belleruth Naparstek's CD **A Meditation To Ease Grief** (see #50, page 132)

111 Things That Help Grieving: **#14**

Grieving on the Installment Plan

At first I was numb functioning on a strange kind of autopilot, calling people, making arrangements, writing her obituary, writing her eulogy, selecting photos, selecting music, and many other chores. It was as if my head was detached from my body, emotions, heart, and my traumatized soul. I did things in those first few months I do not know if I could manage to do today, over four and one half years since her disembodiment. My functioning then seems strangely robotic as I look back on those early days. I am aware without the detachment, denial, repression, and all the other defense mechanisms, I would have been over whelmed beyond the point of survival in the physical realm. Even with all of the defense mechanisms in the service of the ego, I was just hanging on by a thread. Without denial, suppression, repression, dissociation, depersonalization, and all the other defense mechanisms, I would have imploded, exploded, or both. My autopilot functioning served as self protection, providing partial insulation from the intense trauma I experienced with the disembodiment of my beloved.

While I intellectually wanted to "scourge my heart out with honest sorrow,"* the wisdom of my body, mind, soul, and spirit provided an alternative plan. I started to refer to my grieving as grieving on the installment plan or installment grieving. The intensity of loss that has been released from my filtering mechanisms has often seemed far too much to take – raw, dark, heavy with despair and intense longing. My ego mechanisms of defense have protected me, releasing my experience of grief in proportion to my ability to minimally cope. Over time I have come to a greater appreciation of the wisdom of my installment plan style of grieving, as I am sure it could be no other way.

Healing also functions on the installment plan in more or less equal measure with grieving. Bereavement and healing are ongoing with the installment plan being life-long. I do not know how it could be any other way.

---

*Joan Halifax. **Being With Dying: Cultivating Compassion and Fearlessness in the Presence of Death**, Shambhala, 2009, page 192.

111 Things That Help Grieving: **#15**

Triggers

At first, almost anything and everything is a trigger reminding you of the loss of your loved one. Breathing in and out while my disembodied beloved no longer breathes at all. Waking each morning without her beside me on her side of our bed. Going to bed each night missing her physical body beside me. Eating alone. Memories flood - some treasured while others are uninvited and traumatic. Her things. Her smell. Her clothes. Our little cottage we picked out and fixed up together. Presents she gave me. Holidays, anniversaries, birthdays, disembodiment day, and other special days are intense triggers that often start days or weeks before. Driving alone in our car without her beside me. Remembering her smile, laugh, touch, kiss, caress, embrace, and her loving ways. Remembering her warm loving voice. The intense energy of our holding one another. Places we visited together, food we enjoyed, and restaurants we visited. So many triggers. Sometimes it seems life itself triggers attacks of grief, but it is the absence of her embodied person that triggers intense mourning, grieving, tears, heart break, and soul deep pain.

Missing sitting together talking. Sharing our hopes, dreams, fantasies, ideas, thoughts, and experiences. Thinking of things I want to tell her – then remembering. Telling her anyway, often through my tears. Sitting at her shrine. Looking at her black marble urn surrounded by photographs of her and us together across the years. So many shared experiences.

Early on I put away the sick room things. I did not need the sick room paraphernalia to remember her illness. My memories of the last months, weeks, and days were already too intense without the physical presence of her sick room things. I consider this act to be one of my earlier acts of kindness towards myself during my bereavement.

While much has been written about triggers and many examples given, it may be of value to consider the function and benefit of triggers. In the United Sates culture public displays of grief and mourning are not acceptable modes of conduct. Our culture is obsessed with getting on with life and avoiding anything related to dying and death. Many people have incorporated these values, often without conscious awareness, so the function of triggers is to facilitate grieving. To assist in the release of the intense emotions surrounding love and loss. While grieving in public is taboo requiring people to put on their masks of being OK, triggers activate grieving which is a healing function. (Note: If you are early in your grieving, the idea of healing may seem alien, ridiculous. and irritate the hell out of you as it did me for the first several years.) Triggers facilitate grieving, a process I refer to as grieving on the installment plan as few of us have the capacity for a total emotional release. So while triggers are inconvenient when they occur in public settings, they have a positive function. We may need to suppress and control our grieving in public; however, the repression and armoring against the expression of grief in private forces grief "underground" where rather than a healthy release of emotion, the grief accumulates in the body becoming toxic over time.

The most positive reality about triggers is that you experience them. The absence of triggers suggests either the absence of intimate loving relationships or massive denial and repression. While the United States culture may not embrace grief and grieving, your embodied soul grieves and by grieving mindfully you open your heart providing the care and feeding needed by your embodied soul.

You are blessed to have many memories and to have experienced much love. It is intensely sad that with the loss of your beloved you are no longer creating new experiences and new memories to add to your existing triggers. You can have new experiences and create new memories by sharing love across the veil with your disembodied loved one. With the disembodiment of my beloved the best triggers for me are shared golden dreams, her subtle spirit presence, subtle whispers, and inspirations from the other side. These experiences create new memories and new triggers reminding me that love is eternal. Blessings beyond measure.

May the concept and function of triggers be helpful to you in grieving your loss and that you are aware each trigger, while a painful reminder of your loss, is also a reflection of your love. The intensity of your loss is in equal measure to your love. It is further my hope that you are able to develop new memories with your disembodied love one, sharing your love with love flowing freely between the realms. The experience of eternal love is a blessing beyond measure. While always present, eternal love is unfortunately only discovered by some of us after the loss of our embodied loved one.

111 Things That Help Grieving: **#16**

Holidays are hell. Anniversaries are hell. Birthdays are hell. All special days are hell.

Anniversaries, birthdays, and holidays are hell. All special days experienced in the absence of one's physically embodied loved one are intensely painful. Memories, reminisces, and increased distress often start days or weeks before the special date. Especially intense are wedding anniversaries, ones beloved's birthday, and day of disembodiment. One's own birthday without the physical presence of your loved one is just not the same. It has been said that the first full year, a complete cycle of all special days, is the most difficult; however, in my experience years two and three are not significantly better with year four much the same. It does not seem necessary to list all the holidays but some may be more intensely difficult than others – Valentine's Day, Mother's Day, Father's Day, Thanksgiving, Christmas, and New Years. Merchants of all varieties promote holidays and other special days weeks and months before the actual date which create frequent triggers regarding the approaching special day.

Give yourself permission to make major modifications to traditions formerly shared with your now disembodied love one. If possible you can share the history of traditions with family and friends. If not possible to share the history with others, you may write about past special days in your journal as well as your experiences with the current special day. You may be assisted in recapturing a small amount of the emotional memory of the special day by looking at photographs. If you are too raw to look at photographs give yourself permission to set them aside for another time. There is no blame unless it is self inflicted. Give yourself permission to take as much time as you need to adjust to your new reality of your experience in the absence of the physical presence of your embodied love one. There is no race, no finish, no prize, and no gain to rushing.

On special days you can "honor the dead" by setting a place for them at your table. Use your best dishes, glasses, and utensils. Drink a toast to your loved one's spirit presence and in memory of their embodied life. Serve and eat some of your disembodied love one's favorite food. This particular thing that helps grieving may or may not have positive energy for you. You may establish these new traditions and ceremonies if you find them comforting and if not there is no blame.

Awareness that special days are hell will not likely lessen their distress; however, finding ways to observe special days that both honor "the dead" as well as "the living" will start building new traditions. Awareness of the promotion of many holidays and special days will somewhat prepare you for the triggering that happens days and weeks before the actual special day.

In conclusion, no matter how many coping strategies or things that help grieving one implements, anniversaries, birthdays, holidays, and all special days are still hell. It is a hard reality of the experience of love and loss. I do not know how it could be any other way.

111 Things That Help Grieving: **#17**

Regrets and Remorse

Looking back, remembering, and reviewing times and events after the disembodiment of my beloved, I cherish many memories holding them close to my heart. However, other memories are dark and create regrets and remorse. After a time I began to call them errors of commission and errors of omission. Errors of commission are those words and acts that I later regretted having said or done. Errors of omission are those words or acts that I later regretted having not said or done. During the early days, weeks, months, and years remembering and cataloging my errors of commission and omission often accounted for large amounts of time, emotion, and energy. To further complicate the catalogue of regrets and remorse for words and deeds, I added thoughts. In addition to seeing with eyes of love and eyes of loss, I found myself often seeing with eyes of regret and remorse for things I said and did not say; things I did and did not do; and things I thought and did not think. The contrast between seeing with eyes of love and eyes of loss are extreme and intense. Adding seeing with eyes of regret and remorse to my life review has intensified my experience of the hellfires of grief.

Several concepts have helped me in my struggle with errors of commission and omission. I realize that comparing my embodied self to my higher self, or my ideal self, is an experience of which I will most certainly fall far short. To quote Carol Susan,

"The biggest part of it is about forgiveness." Forgiveness for being less than my higher self or my ideal self. Forgiveness for being a flawed embodied being with imperfections - more lead than gold. So to quote Carol Susan again, I have done the best I could "within my limitations." And so it will have to be good enough. Now and then I find I almost accept my limitations and the imperfections of my embodied being. More often I find myself in the alchemical fires of transformation slowly burning away the lead of imperfection with glimpses of the alchemical gold of the spirit realm.

111 Things That Help Grieving: **#18**

Death as Advisor/Death as Companion

In the early 1970's reading Carlos Castaneda's' book **Journey to Ixtlan: The Lessons of Don Juan,** I was very taken with Chapter 4: Death Is An Advisor.* I adopted the image of death as always just behind my left shoulder and when it was my time death would reach out and tap me on the shoulder. Don Juan told Carlos that if you looked around quickly sometimes you could get a glimpse of your death stalking you. I talked about this image for years. After the disembodiment of my beloved Carol Susan, I realized all of those years of maintaining death as my advisor had been an intellectual exercise. The concept and image never dropped out of my head and into my center – my heart of hearts.

I no longer think about death as my advisor. I now know death as my constant companion. My image is of an invisible black bone scarf draped around my neck and hanging down into my center- my heart of hearts. Before, I intellectually understood the impermanence of the physical body as physical realm lives are vulnerable and short lived. After Carol Susan's disembodiment, I have a much deeper understanding – a knowing of the delicate nature of physical realm life and the apparent randomness of each life span. The chaos created by my loss has moved physical realm death from my head to my heart. I can no longer pretend that I have any understanding of the mysteries of life and death and certainly no control.

Another concept that I have long quoted but not often followed is a saying by Chuang Tau translated by Lin Yutang:

"Only those who take leisurely what the people of the world are busy about can be busy about what the people of the world take leisurely."**

Another intellectual exercise. A lovely concept which I have long understood in my head but unfortunately not always practiced. Too often busy chasing the gold ring or other shiny bobble.

Death as my companion whispers when I become sidetracked and preoccupied with the trappings and possessions of the physical realm forgetting my soul's purpose. The trauma of major loss breaks the heart and a broken heart is an open heart. A broken open heart is the way I have experienced death transforming from an advisor to death as my constant companion. A very painful way to discover the difference between my intellectual knowing; which is why I often ignored my advisor as my priorities were elsewhere; and the heart level experience of loss, when death no longer advises but lives within my heart as a mysterious companion.

*Carlos Castaneda. ***Journey to Itxlan: The Lessons of Don Juan***. Simon and Schuster, 1972, chapter 4: Death Is An Advisor, pages 46-57.

Lin Yutang. **The Importance of Living. Harper, 1937/1965/1996, page 323.

111 Things That Help Grieving: **#19**

Widower/Widow

According to the law, after the disembodiment of my beloved my legal status became that of a widower. The Division of Motor Vehicles would not issue new tags for my automobiles on line, I had to show up in person and surrender the joint titles so I could be reissued titles in my name only. At the time I was in shock and denial so my reaction to the DMV requirement was one of disbelief and anguish. Intellectually I understood that they already had identified my beloved as deceased from the filing of her death certificate but emotionally I was not ready for the change from our cars to my cars. Same was true of filing income tax designated as a single person. The bank modified my accounts from joint to single. The new checks in my name only became another reminder of the reality of my experience. As the examples suggest, the culture converted me to widowerhood in a very rapid and in what seemed to me a heartless fashion. I was heartbroken by the disembodiment of my beloved and did not want to be constantly reminded of my new legal status, yet at what seemed like at almost every turn, I was confronted by my new label of widower.

I do not like my legal status of widower and while I know it to be true in physical realm reality, I also know that my connection to my beloved transcends physical realm embodiment. The paradox of my widowerhood is that I understand my legal status in the physical realm but I do not feel disconnected from my beloved. The connection is far more subtle and while I intensely miss my physically embodied loved one, our connection continues in the spirit realm and is also experienced in the physical realm in subtle ways. Legally I may be a widower in the physical realm but my heart of hearts knows love is always, forever, and beyond – eternal.

Do not allow your legal status to overrule the wisdom of your heart of hearts. Your heart of hearts knows that the connections between loved ones does not end with the disembodiment of one or the other but continues uninterrupted just in a more subtle form. May you be blessed to remember golden dreams and other messages from your disembodied love one and that you are able to maintain your connection to your disembodied loved one without regard to your legal status in the physical realm.

111 Things That Help Grieving: **#20**

Complicated Grief/Complicated Bereavement

My first reaction to the concept of complicated grief is "how could it be any other way?" Perhaps not a helpful response; however, the loss of a loved one is one of the most complicated and stressful experiences of a lifetime and often **the** most complicated and stressful experience of a lifetime. The closer and more intense the relationship, the more intense and complicated the grief with the disembodiment of a loved one. If you are blessed with golden dreams and other messages from your disembodied love one, your grief becomes much more complicated as the grief of your loss in the physical realm is contrasted with your ongoing connection to your beloved in the spirit realm. The contrast is what I refer to as seeing with eyes of loss versus seeing with eyes of love. The physical connection is dramatically diminished with the disembodiment of your loved one as the spirit realm connection becomes prominent and over time perhaps primary providing the healing energies of eternal love.

In the first few years of my bereavement, I was mostly focused on the loss of my embodied companion. At the level of my heart of hearts I was aware that a portion of my embodied soul disembodied with my beloved to accompany my beloved to our spirit realm home. I was diminished by the loss of my embodied soulmate as well as by the disembodiment of those aspects of my embodied soul who returned with her to the spirit realm. Achieving a balance between the experiences of loss in the physical realm and the ongoing connection in the spirit realm is a complex process. In my experience, eyes of loss often prevail while eyes of love provide the healing golden energy of eternal love.

I am aware that my use of the concept of complicated grief is not the conventional usage; however, the conventional concept adds little, if any, value to those who are experiencing the loss of a loved one. The concept suggests a certain time allotted to "get over" the loss of a loved one. The concept of complicated grief, used as a clinical term, reinforces the cultural value that grief and grieving should be brief, mostly private, and recovery – often termed resilience – should be sooner than later. If the loss of a loved one results in clinical depression then treatment for a major depressive disorder is indicated. (see sadness and depression, #21) When grief is complicated with a coexisting condition of depression, the addition of the concept of complicated grief does not add value. The coexistence of grief and depression is complication enough without the need for the label of complicated bereavement. The label of complicated grief only adds a negative value to the experience of loss particularly when used in the absence of symptoms of a major depressive disorder.

My initial reaction to the concept of complicated grief remains unchanged – "how could it be any other way?" May you be able to honor your disembodied love ones as well as honoring the living without regard for nor accepting the negative label of complicated grief. Of course grief is complicated, how could it be any other way? If you are experiencing the signs and symptoms of a major depressive disorder coexisting with your grief, seek assistance from medical, mental health, and other helping/healing professionals.

111 Things That Help Grieving: **#21**

Sadness and Depression

Sadness is a mood. Depression is a mood disorder. Sadness is one of the natural human emotions resulting from loss, the greater the loss the greater the emotion of sadness. Depression is a clinical term indicating a pathological condition in need of treatment. Words have power. The casual use of the word "depression" to refer to a condition of sadness, even chronic sadness, may appear a minor semantic matter; however, labeling a natural human emotion a pathological mood disorder may become a self fulfilling prophesy. It seems that in everyday use many consider the two words equivalent. Currently the use of the word "sadness" does not appear in vogue nor able to communicate the intensity of one's mood.

While there is a tendency to equate grief to depression considering the clinical indicators for depression may provide improved clarity regarding the difference between sadness and depression. The American Psychiatric Association (APA) in their **DSM-5 Fact Sheet: Major Depressive Disorder and the "Bereavement Exclusion"** (2013, page 1) notes:

"While the grieving process is natural and unique to each individual and shares some of the same features of depression like intense sadness and withdrawal from customary activities, grief and depression are also different in important aspects:

- In grief, painful feelings come in waves, often intermixed with positive memories of the deceased; in depression, mood and ideation are almost constantly negative.
- In grief, self-esteem is usually preserved; in MDD (*major depressive disorder*), corrosive feelings of worthlessness and self-loathing are common.
- While many believe that some form of depression is a normal consequence of bereavement, MDD (*major depressive disorder*) should not be diagnosed in the context of bereavement since diagnosis would incorrectly label a normal process as a disorder."

The APA DSM-5 Fact Sheet also indicates: "The presence of symptoms such as feelings of worthlessness, suicidal ideas (as distinct from wanting to join a deceased loved one), and impairment of overall function suggest the presence of major depression, in addition to the normal response to a significant loss." (page 2)

The APA's fact sheet further notes that "...the death of a loved one can precipitate major depression...when grief and depression coexist, the grief is more severe and prolonged than grief without major depression. Despite some overlap between grief and MDD (*major depressive disorder*), they are different in important ways, and therefore they should be distinguished separately to enable people to benefit from the most appropriate treatment." (page 1)

The natural human response to the loss of a loved one is the emotion of sadness – intense, overwhelming, heartbreaking sadness. Sadness is not depression. Should you have the symptoms of a major depressive disorder, seek the assistance of medical and behavioral health (mental health) professionals.

"Then turn to the dead, listen to their lament and accept them with love."

C.G. Jung

Section Two

Activities Actions Doing

As part of the grieving process, there are times when the need, impulse, and inspiration to take action – to do something – becomes overwhelmingly compelling. The focus of many activities is to honor the disembodied loved one ("the dead"). Activities, actions, and doing that honor the disembodied also honor grieving embodied souls ("the living"). Honoring and venerating disembodied loved ones maintains the energy connections that have become more subtle, now existing across realms. Activities to maintain the energy connection provides a flowing of the healing energies of love between beings of spirit and embodied souls. In the alchemy of grief, ceremonies and other activities that take place in the physical realm also take place in the heart of hearts providing essential elements of the alchemical grief process of transformation.

111 Things That Help Grieving: **#22**

Honoring the Dead

"Then turn to the dead, listen to their lament and accept them with love."*

C.G. Jung

"To outward appearances, endings are a structural matter-now there is a relationship, now there is not a relationship. From the soul point of view, ending is a different experience of the relationship. Ending is not literal at all, but is rather a radical shift in imagination. ...In this respect it is important to honor the dead, especially those with whom we have a close relationship. The soul is not limited in its experience to the confinements of life. Death doesn't erase a relationship, it simply places it in a different context. Fostering our relationships to the dead gives the soul its nourishment of eternity, melancholy, mystery, and the kind of relatedness that is not literally of this world. Many, many stories of the soul tell that it is not fully at home in this life and that it is always trying to break the bonds of this world's limitations. We can honor the soul by nurturing our relationships with the dead, whether by visiting and decorating their graves, by praying for them when their memories drift into mind, by naming our children after them, by preserving and using objects they've left behind, or by telling their stories and keeping photographs and paintings of them within sight. ...One radical difference between care of soul and a great deal of modern psychological work is that the former offers a profound appreciation for the personalities who are important in our lives, even if they are flawed people and even if the relationship is not perfect. Psychology prefers to analyze with the goal of increased understanding, yet understanding does little for the soul. Imagine telling stories of the dead, not for insight into ourselves, but simply to establish a deep, continuing relationship with them. The soul is given eternity in that exchange, while understanding offers it little more that another fragment of logic that has nothing to do with establishing a home for the infinite within our finite lives....It isn't a question, anyway, of deciding whether we should or should not give attention to the dead. They present themselves to us in unsought memories, in dreams, and in momentary visitations during the day or night."**

Thomas Moore

"The dead" lament because they are not being honored by "the living." I prefer to call "the dead" "the disembodied." "The dead" are not dead rather transformed and reunited with their higher forms in the spirit realm. There are many ways to honor "the dead." Both the living and the dead benefit from these honoring activities. The embodied soul is nourished by the ongoing relationship with the disembodied loved one and the disembodied love one has less need to lament if they are being acknowledged and honored. There are many activities and ways to honor the dead, some of which will be listed briefly and expanded in separate things that help grieving. Honoring the last wishes of the dead is an essential way of honoring the dead. Establishing a shrine. Being open to whispers, inspirations, and other messages from the disembodied. The communications may come in dreams including day dreams. Setting aside time each day to communicate with your disembodied loved one(s). Developing ways to observe special days that honor the disembodied love one. Ceremonies that mark special days, as well as every other day, maintain the energetic connection between the disembodied ("the dead") and the embodied ("the living"). Talking with the dead and listening to their response. Many wisdom traditions honor the ancestors in many ways including telling stories about them, setting a place for them at the table, and using their possessions (understanding intuitively that the objects retain residual energy). Honoring the dead by displaying photographs of them. Establishing a memorial of some kind depending on one's circumstances. A memorial can be planting a small tree even if you are not a land holder – a tree in a public area or park can be planted or donated for planting.

The details of "honoring the dead" are less critical than the concept of maintaining a continuing relationship with one's disembodied loved ones. Depending on style and intuition each individual can establish an ongoing relationship and communication with their dead. Being open to the whispering of one's own soul will provide inspiration about how to honor the dead.

The concept of honoring the dead may seem alien to some individuals raised in a death adverse culture. As Thomas Moore has eloquently expressed, one's embodied soul needs to honor the dead as much as the dead need to be honored – perhaps even more so. Establishing ways to honor the dead is essential in transforming the focus from loss to eternal love. People speak about the presence of their departed loved ones, so the concept is part of our intuitive knowing, even if the logical rational culture ridicules the concept and practices of honoring the dead. I suspect many people honor the dead in private ceremonies, in day to day private conversations, and in many other ways that are not shared with "the living."

If you have been uncertain about how to honor your disembodied loved one, follow your heart and soul, listen for messages, and if you are still uncertain establish a shrine if only one photograph or one flower.

---

*C.G. Jung, **The Red Book: Liber Novus: A Reader's Edition**, WW Norton, 2009, page xx.

Thomas Moore, **Soul Mates: Honoring the Mysteries of Love and Relationship, Harper Collins, 1994, pages 200-203.

111 Things That Help Grieving: **#23**

Honoring Last Requests/Last Wishes

The last requests or last wishes of a disembodied love one are sacred requests that need to be honored. Honoring the last requests of your beloved honors them, honors your love, and honors your embodied soul for whom such last requests are a sacred trust. Honoring the last requests of my beloved provides me with an ongoing way of demonstrating my love and sending my love to her. Honoring last requests is an act of loving kindness both for your loved one as well as for yourself.

Last requests can take many forms and are often acts of loving kindness from your loved one. Carol Susan and I were walking in a public garden she had always enjoyed when she pointed to the memorial flagstones that made up the path. She told me she wanted one. Through my tears I agreed. Of course I honored her request and the garden now has her memorial flagstone among the others. I visit it now and then and find the visits to be a very emotional experience. I am not at all sure Carol Susan really wanted the memorial flagstone. It was one of the ways she was preparing me for her disembodiment. At the time of her request I was in massive denial and not ready to consider her disembodiment, even though I had researched her diagnosis and intellectually understood her extremely short remaining life expectancy. I expect the reason her memorial flagstone is so emotional for me is it reminds me of one of her many acts of loving kindness across many years and specifically her loving ways to prepare me for the time her physical form could no longer support or contain her beautiful radiant spirit.

Another of Carol Susan's last requests was to honor her mother and grandmother by providing books to the schools in the village where her mother grew up. Family, friends, and colleagues worked to honor this request providing several large deliveries of books with more delivers anticipated.

I suspect many last requests are generated at the level of the embodied soul, who is aware of the short time remaining; therefore, many last requests are at the soul's level of wisdom.

Should your loved one have not communicated their last requests, I suggest being open to inspirations about their last requests and honor the last requests you receive by inspiration.

With each last request honored, the connection between the physical realm and spirit realm is strengthened. Your embodied soul will be grateful as will your disembodied loved one.

111 Things That Help Grieving: **#24**

Naming Grief/Image of Grief

When I became less than in total shock and denial, I had the image of my experience of grief as riding on the tail of a huge dragon. Just holding on being whipped about wildly. Later, I climbed up towards the head of the dragon, I named grief, sitting on its neck trying to steer the beast with no success. Then I decided to enter the dragon named grief, so I jumped into the mouth of the dragon to be swallowed alive. At the same time, I experienced the image of swallowing the dragon. So paradoxically, I was in the belly of the dragon named grief and simultaneously the dragon named grief was in my stomach. Curiously this image provided a measure of comfort. I determined that it would take a very long time for me to work my way through the digestive system of the dragon named grief and it would take an equally long time for me to digest the dragon named grief I had swallowed. I imagined myself eventually emerging from the rear end of the dragon. Being born from the dragon named grief in an unconventional manner. No longer the same as when I entered the dragon and with the smell of the dragon named grief permeating my physical being. I can only speculate about being born from the dragon named grief as I am still somewhere inside of the beast as I write this thing that helps grieving.

Naming my grief and the image of the dragon named grief did not over power the dragon named grief but the image of jumping into the mouth of the dragon was helpful and marked a time when I decided to no longer ride on the tail of the beast but encounter the monster head first. The companion image of swallowing the dragon named grief was also a very powerful image/concept for me. The image of being inside the dragon named grief was the size of the impact of my loss and grief. The image of swallowing the dragon named grief was my attempt to digest the monster as best I could. I can also not tell you about the end result of my digesting the grief monster. I do know that swallowing the dragon named grief and slowly digesting the beast has permeated every cell of my physical body as well as several layers of subtle energy bodies.

At some point I became aware that the naming of my grief "a dragon named grief" was not a real or proper name. It then occurred to me that the dragon named grief's name was Carlos Eldon – the same as my name Charles Eldon yet the Spanish version Carol Susan had christened me with long ago saying it was a better fit. This awareness and new proper name for the dragon named grief was a very powerful awareness – not an intellectual concept – but a deeper subtle knowing in my heart of hearts. The dragon named grief was me and not a dragon from otherwhere but the dragon named grief is part of me with the name Carlos Eldon. The dragon is part of my being. The accumulated energy of my love and loss and grief at the level of my embodied soul – the heart of my hearts.

The progression of images: riding on the tail, working my way to the head, sitting on the neck, trying to control the monster with no success, until the moment I decided to jump into the mouth and belly of the beast describes different aspects of my grief journey. Not to control grief but to leap into the mouth of grief – to encounter grief fully (as fully as I can manage) and eventually to emerge from the tail end of the beast different from the person who jumped into the mouth so many years ago. The process of digesting the dragon is also an image that I have found to be one of the things that help. In the one image, I am digesting the dragon named grief from within and in the other image, the dragon named grief is transforming me as I drop ever lower into the center of the beast. Curiously the dragon named grief is unable to digest me even though I am within and, of course, the awareness that the dragon named grief's name is my own provides the reason. The dragon is one aspect of myself. As I digest the dragon named grief within, I am also transforming the dragon from within. I now intuit that I will not be born from the tail end of the dragon named grief after all. I now suspect that I will slowly transform into the golden rainbow dragon named Carlos Eldon. Not the energy being's real name but close enough for now.

Embracing the dragon named grief and discovering its name is the same as mine – not an intellectual discovery – a discovery of my heart of hearts has been a transformational awareness. At first the dragon named grief took up the entire landscape as very little else existed. This was when my focus was almost exclusively looking from the eyes of loss. After my experiences with golden dreams and other subtle messages, the dragon named grief started to slowly reveal its golden edges and reveal the slightest hint of its rainbow nature. Over time, I came to see with both the eyes of loss (the black dragon named grief) and the eyes of love (the golden rainbow dragon). The dragon named grief obscured the golden rainbow dragon since I was too traumatized by the loss of my beloved to see with any other eyes than eyes of loss.

111 Things That Help Grieving: **#25**

Life Review

Wisdom traditions describe the newly disembodied soul arriving at a particular location and tasked with conducting a review of their embodied life. This is usually presented as happening after crossing over and being welcomed by family, friends, and others. The spirit realm life review is not the only life review that takes place. Those left behind often find themselves involved with a life review of their own.

The life review experience that occurs after the disembodiment of a loved one involves examining errors of omission in word and deed. Things you did not say and now wish you had said and things you did not do and now wish you had done. Another major area of the life review experience is examining errors of commission in word and deed. Things you said and now wish you had not and things you did and now wish you had not done. The life review process can involve considerable remorse, guilt, and shame. For some this soul searching is omitted as the person shrinks from the task of an honest assessment of their strengths and weaknesses. For those with the personal courage to conduct a life review, the process will have a positive healing effect – eventually. It is not an easy process and is often a major part of the experience of the dark night of the soul. The burning in the hellfires of grief as a result of your loss also results in an intense focus on your shared moments with your now disembodied loved one, the good, bad, and perhaps awful.

In encountering your life review, it may be helpful to remember that your emotional condition is raw, dark, and heavy. The loss has broken open your heart and; if you tend to be self-critical; your self assessment may be unrealistically harsh. Most people have done the very best they could within their limitations. So acknowledging and accepting ones limitations becomes one of the goals of the embodied live review. This is the time for extending compassion and forgiveness towards oneself. Extending compassion and forgiveness towards your departed loved one may also be an important goal of your life review. They very likely also did the very best they could within their limitations.

While the life review may start with the dark side, with errors of omission and commission, as the process continues the development of increased compassion, forgiveness, and acceptance of yourself in the awareness that you most likely did the very best your could do within your limitations opens the life review process to the positive side. The life review then includes your acts of kindness, caring, and love. Contrary to the wisdom traditions which suggest the spirit realm life review is completed relatively quickly for most disembodied spirits; the life review process for those still embodied is likely more long term if not a lifelong process.

May your life review process includes large measures of compassion and forgiveness for any and all errors of omission and commission. That you are able to acknowledge and accept that you did the best you could within your limitations. Most important is you send your love and receive love from your disembodied love one. Maintaining your connection to your love one on the other side enriches both you and your disembodied love one.

111 Things That Help Grieving: **#26**

Ceremonies

Establishing ceremonies is an essential way to honor your disembodied loved one, provide a measure of comfort to your broken heart, and honor your embodied soul. The culture provides very few ceremonies and usually only during the early days after the loss. A funeral and/or memorial service and a few functions with family and friends after which many find themselves left to grieve alone. Those who have family and friends who continue to provide support are blessed in great measure.

Ceremonies provide a time, place, and activities for remembering and expressing your ongoing love as well as your grief. Many of the things that help are focused on elements of ceremony. When you have a ceremony, one of the first things that needs to happen is to switch from day to day activities to your intent to conduct a ceremony. Your intent to conduct a ceremony allows you to create a sacred space where you transcend ordinary reality, parting the veil, and experiencing the spirit realm. You may not consciously create a sacred space; however, your intent to honor your loved one generates a sacred space. Creating sacred space consciously offers additional awareness and comfort. It is not difficult to create sacred space as all is required is your sincere intent to conduct a ceremony. Many wisdom traditions have formal ways to create sacred space. You can adopt one of these or create your own.

Establishing a shrine provides an excellent location to conduct ceremonies. The shrine can be as elaborate as you can imagine or as simple as a single photograph. Once you have established a shrine, you have a location to sit and focus on your loss, send your love to your disembodied loved one, and receive their love in return.

I start my ceremonies by lighting incense. I burn the incense outside as the smoke is intended to rise beyond the physical realm and enter the spirit realm. I light candles at the shrine. On special days I share black water and on extra special days I share cognac. I play special music that vibrates in both realms. Each evening I sit at the shrine and write in my journal. I also write poems and things that help grieving at the shrine. The shrine is crowded with photos of my beloved, a perpetually blooming purple orchid, and copies of the books of poems I have written after the disembodiment of my beloved.

When traveling a portable shrine can be no more than a single photograph. It is enough. Sacred space is within the heart of hearts and expands to create the golden energy of the spirit realm.

A note on ceremony and ritual:
I associate the term "ritual" with an automatic practice or habit often lacking the energy of sacred space. Going through the motions. In the extreme

ritual becomes dysfunctional even pathological. I am aware that others do not share my definition. For me, a ceremony takes place by transforming ordinary reality into sacred space while rituals are conducted in ordinary reality.

I suspect you have created and are already conducting ceremonies. Even if you have not called those times where you stop to remember, look at photos, or sit holding an object of your disembodied loved one a ceremony; you have created and entered sacred space and are conducting a ceremony. If you have not created nor conducted regular ceremonies, I hope in describing ceremonies you will be inspired to create and conduct your own ceremonies. May you experience your ceremonies as portals to the spirit realm and experience loving energies flowing in both directions. Ceremonies are one of the ways to slowly transcend from seeing only with eyes of loss to also seeing with eyes of love – eternal love.

Note: The things that help grieving that follow amplify aspects of ceremony with the intent of providing concepts, ideas, and activities to consider for your ceremonies (see #27 – #37, pages 80-98).

111 Things That Help Grieving: **#27**

Moratorium on Holidays

If your loved one disembodied on or near a holiday, the loss will make it very difficult, if not impossible, to observe the holiday much less celebrate. Unless there are compelling reasons (young children or young grandchildren), I suggest considering declaring a moratorium on the holiday. Actually no matter the date of your loved ones disembodiment, you may find all holidays (and other special days such as birthdays and anniversaries) to be painful reminders of the reality of your experience as your beloved is no longer physically present to share in holiday traditions. Therefore, I suggest you consider suspending holidays at least until you can develop a way to observe the holiday that also honors your disembodied loved one.

My beloved disembodied on October 31st which is Halloween and Samhain with the next day (November 1st) being All Saints Day and the Day of the Dead followed by All Souls Day (November 2nd). I no longer observe or celebrate Halloween or Samhain as I have renamed October 31st Disembodiment Day. I observe Disembodiment Day with a number of ceremonies to honor my "dead" as well as a few of my "living."

Consider some version of a moratorium on holidays, should this idea have positive energy or appeal for you. Should your loved one have disembodied on or near a holiday or other special day that day will be all the more emotionally distressing. For most holidays merchants start displaying their holiday wares months in advance. Halloween "season" now starts in September. For the first few years, I found the Halloween displays quite distressing. Now, four and one half years post-disembodiment day, I still do not like Halloween displays but now say to myself "It is not Halloween for me, it is Disembodiment Day." I am happy for others who can enjoy Halloween/Samhain, I just do not participate.

111 Things That Help Grieving: **#28**

Maintaining Traditions

I continue to maintain some of the traditions established while Carol Susan and I were embodied together. I have not maintained many traditions associated with holidays and other special days. Holidays and other special days are filled with loving memories and many wonderful traditions that can no longer be celebrated with my embodied soulmate. I observe holidays and other special days with new traditions that honor my disembodied loved one and honor our embodied lives together. The new traditions include burning incense, lighting candles, sharing black water and cognac, spending time reminiscing remembering traditions, and giving myself permission not to maintain many of our traditions we shared embodied together.

I have maintained some traditions we shared and have continued some of Carol Susan's traditions in her memory and on her behalf. Holidays and special days were celebrated for many years creating many traditions we shared embodied together. An act of loving kindness that I have given to myself is not to attempt to carry on most of these special traditions. Holidays and other special days are difficult enough without feeling the pressure of maintaining the many traditions we shared embodied together. Extending permission to myself to no longer maintain these special traditions reduces the distress of holidays and special days which are more than distressing enough without maintaining traditions once shared embodied together, filled with loving energy then but now are often reminders of loss.

Give yourself permission to not feel obligated to maintain all of the traditions once shared with your embodied loved one. Create new traditions that honor your disembodied loved one and your lives shared embodied together. Maintain those traditions that bring a measure of comfort, solace, and healing energy while discontinuing those traditions that are too distressing to maintain. To use the words of the **I Ching** there is no harm - no blame to not maintaining traditions that do not bring healing energy. It is essential to maintain those traditions that continue to have healing energy as well as establishing new traditions which bring the healing energy of honoring your disembodied loved one and your lives shared embodied together.

111 Things That Help Grieving: **#29**

Grief Work

Grieving is painful hard work. The loss of a loved one is one of the most traumatic experiences of an embodied lifetime. The loss of a beloved spouse, soulmate, companion best friend, and partner **is the** most traumatic experience.

Everyone grieves even if their grieving is underground – meaning they are engaged in massive denial and repression of their loss and the resulting grief. Everyone needs the protection of denial and disbelief, so grief and grieving is experienced as if on the installment plan. Little by little the harsh painful reality comes into sharper and ever more painful focus. Installment plan grieving is a protective function so the trauma of the loss can be slowly encountered. The full magnitude of loss, if faced head on, would likely prove overwhelming and life threatening. Anecdotal evidence suggests that grief can result in death, even though grief is not listed as the cause of death.

The loss of your loved one creates a huge black hole in the middle of your life and in the middle of your heart. Even your embodied soul is in mourning. The loss further creates or intensifies the quest for answers to complex metaphysical questions. If you are already a seeker, which I suspect may be the case, then your seeking, like mine, has likely intensified from part-time to an intense full-time search, at first for answers and then to improved connection to the spirit realm. Questions about purpose, mission, and meaning of this embodied life also intensify. I suspect that you may have also embarked on a life review as part of your grief work.

As your beloved has graduated from the school of this physical realm existence then why and for what reason(s) and purpose(s) are you still here? The one left behind still has work to do, people to support, and tasks to accomplish. The one who has gone ahead may be able to help, but the work of honoring the dead, supporting the living, reevaluating your life, discovering your soul's mission and purpose, and coping with the loss is complex and intense work of the embodied one remaining in the physical realm. While grief work is a labor of love, it does not lessen the trauma or the pain. Grief work most likely involves a decent into the heart of the pain and into the black night of the soul. If you are fortunate, you will discover helpers in both the physical realm and spirit realm to assist you to expand the reality of your experience across dimensions.

I do not want to suggest that the school of life has report cards nor that there is such a thing as "good grief." I do suggest that conscious and mindful grieving is much more likely to result in reaching a transformational level where eyes of loss are balanced with eyes of love. Grief work continues beyond that balance into the realm of eternal love and yet eyes of loss remain. It is the paradox of the reality of experience with physical realm loss existing side by side with eternal love.

If you are early in your grieving, the idea of transformation likely sounds ridiculous, if not absurd. I felt the same way for any number of years, so as the **I Ching** advises no harm no blame.

111 Things That Help Grieving: **#30**

Memories/Reminisces

After the disembodiment of my beloved, many of my memories and reminisces were dark as I relived her illness and last years. My memories of her last days were beyond dark and were often my primary focus. My memories dwelt on loss as I looked through eyes of loss. Over time, I began to remember loving moments shared with my embodied loved one. Golden dreams provided new experiences, memories, and moments for reminisces. Golden dreams have provided the most powerful healing experiences, as they not only reawaken memories of love shared together, they also provide the experience that our love continues to be shared only in a different form. Even during the blackest times, golden dreams helped reawaken my memory of the love shared with my embodied soulmate. Slowly seeing and remembering with eyes of love became more frequent and strengthened by golden dreams coexisting with the dark memories. After years of dark memories of illness and loss prevailing, memoires of a life time of love shared embodied now often over whelm the black memories. Golden dreams and other subtle experiences provide new loving memories and the energy to transform the black nights into golden memories.

This is not to suggest that the dark memories and reminisces have disappeared, rather that they have lost some of their prominence and no longer prevail. There was a moment when I realized I was spending about equal time remembering the dark experiences and the golden moments. This awareness of the transformation towards balance was a revelation with powerful healing energy. The awareness that new loving golden memories were being created provides powerful healing energy. The ability to look beyond the time spent with my embodied beloved to the ongoing experiences of our loving connection which has created wonderful new memories, which I treasure beyond words. Of course, not all dreams are golden dreams, as many are what I term housekeeping dreams where I continue to burn away the impurities of my being as I work to realize my essential nature and the essences of my soul. Other dreams, like some memories, are black nightmares where I remember and re-experience the dark times.

The balance of golden dreams and loving memories to black dreams and black memories has slowly shifted over time. With active grief work, meaning embracing grieving, the balance towards loving experiences can be expedited. Expedited does not mean the black memories and nightmares disappear, but no longer prevail as they are slowly over whelmed by golden dreams, loving experiences, and loving memories.

May you remember your experiences shared with your disembodied loved one in golden dreams and other subtle experiences. May you experience the transformation of your embodied love one into their disembodied spirit form and experience the love you shared embodied now transformed into the eternal love of your higher selves experienced in your spirit realm home.

111 Things That Help Grieving: **#31**

Establishing A Shrine

"We can be initiated and educated by moments of torment, if only we place a flower at its shine, or spill some wine to honor that very place in our intimacy that has been painfully opened for our contemplation and attention."*
Thomas Moore

Establishing a shrine creates a sacred space creating a connection between the physical realm and spirit realm. The shrine can be very small – a single small photograph or very elaborate spreading out over considerable space. The shrine can be portable, traveling with you consisting of a small photograph or a more elaborate collection of special things. When I established a shrine to honor my disembodied beloved, I started with a two foot by three foot photograph from the memorial service and the black marble urn holding her ashes. Next I added favorite photographs, candles, and a constantly blooming purple orchid (requires periodic replacement). I have a comfortable chair in front of the shrine and a small table where I keep my journal. At the end of each day I light incense (outside), light a candle, and play special music as I sit at the shrine and write in my journal. On special days I share black water and cognac. The shrine continues to expand into surrounding walls with photographs and drawers with special objects.

The size and composition of the shrine is less important than establishing a sacred focal point. The true shrine is within our heart of hearts – the embodied soul of each person who creates a shrine. Sitting at the shrine observing special days offers a measure of comfort.

If you do not have a shrine, consider establishing a shrine no matter how small. Perhaps you already have a special photograph in which you find comfort having nearby. You may not call it a shrine. Should you wish to keep your shrine private, it can be established in a drawer. Creating a shrine establishes a sacred space that will facilitate communication with the spirit realm. The communications may be quite subtle – whispers, inspirations, and loving energy. Sitting at your shrine may provide a measure of solace not found elsewhere.

---

*Thomas Moore **Soul Mates: Honoring the Mysteries of Love and Relationship**, Harper Collins, 1994, page 229.

111 Things That Help Grieving: #32

Elements at the Shrine

In keeping with many wisdom traditions, I maintain the elements of earth, water, air, and fire at the shrine. Earth is represented by the live purple orchid, black marble urn, and the ashes of my beloved. Water is represented by sharing black water and cognac on special occasions. A water bottle is always present. My tears add additional water. Fire is represented by candles and the intense emotion of bereavement. The element air is represented by my breathing and the painful awareness that my disembodied loved one no longer breathes physical realm air. The incense, which I consider part of the shrine, even though remote, adds fire and smoke. Lighting incense starts the ceremony of sitting at the shrine. I also add food from time to time on special occasions. Sharing black water, cognac, and food is part of my ceremony honoring my disembodied loved one and is a variation of ceremony practiced by many wisdom traditions. See sharing quintessence (#67) for additional information.

If you have not established a shrine, I hope sharing information about the ceremonies and shrine I have developed to honor my disembodied loved one provides you with ideas you can incorporate in honoring your loved one. Conventional wisdom does not support honoring the dead in ongoing ceremonies which is both tragic and easily remedied. Your soul will be nourished by your activities that honor your dead and your disembodied loved one will have much less reason to lament. Honoring the dead enables enriching both "the living" and "the dead."

111 Things That Help Grieving: **#33**

Flowers at the Shrine

Placing a flower at the shrine to honor your disembodied loved one is an ancient wisdom tradition. The flower may be a cut flower or a live flowering plant. I prefer a live plant at the shrine honoring my beloved. Her shrine always has a purple orchid in bloom. I replace the old orchid when the blooms fall off with a new one in full bloom. Having a live green blooming plant at the shrine provides comfort to me and communicates my ongoing love. I add cut flowers from time to time, often from the garden. In the fall I add colored leaves to the shrine and remember sharing the seasons with my beloved when were embodied together. We continue to share the seasons; however, she is in a more subtle form. Her physical eyes no longer witness the shrine but I know her spirit vision does.

If you have not included flowers as part of your shrine, consider adding flowers to your shrine. The falling orchid blooms remind me of the transient nature of our physical realm existence while my heart of heart looks into the eternity of our spirit realm existence.

111 Things That Help Grieving: **#34**

Lighting Candles

Many wisdom traditions light candles as part of their ceremonies. Lighting candles marks the start of the ceremony and extinguishing candles marks the end. Lighting candles creates sacred space and communicates the intent of honoring the disembodied loved one.

I add a different colored candle for each year. For year one the candle is black, year two purple, year three amber/gold, and year four white. For some time I would light all the candles but after I adopted my cat, her interest in the flames required that I light only one and monitor it closely.

Candles add the element of fire to the shrine. If you do not currently light a candle at your shrine you might consider adding a candle. You could light the candle on special days and only burn it while near your shrine. If you are concerned about the risk, you could use a candle enclosed in a safe container.

111 Things That Help Grieving: **#35**

Burning Incense

Many wisdom traditions incorporate burning incense as part of their ceremonies. Incense adds the elements of fire and air to ceremonies with the smoke honoring the dead. The quintessence of the incense crosses the divide between the physical and spirit realms sending loving energy to our spirit loved ones. After the disembodiment of my beloved, I burned incense all day and most of the night. I used very large incense at the end of the day so the incense burned for a good portion of the night. I selected a black container filled it with fine black gravel and placed it outside on the porch on a small table. I light incense each evening before I sit down to write in my journal. The incense helps to create a sacred space along with lighting candles, playing music, and sharing black water and cognac (on special occasions). Burning incense is a part of my ceremonies that "honor the dead" sending my love to my disembodied beloved. Watching the smoke rise and disappear provides a focus for communications across realms. For the first six months or so I burned incense all day and most all night. At the time of this writing (four years and one half years) I burn incense once a day except for special days when I burn extra incense.

If you have not tried burning incense as part of your ceremonies consider lighting incense on special days. Incense is another way of honoring the dead and sending your loving energy to them.

111 Things That Help Grieving: **#36**

Photographs

Looking at photographs of happier times is a painful reminder of loss and can trigger intense grief. Looking at photographs also brings the energy of love, reminding us of cherished moments shared with our disembodied loved one. I have photographs in albums and computer files; however, the photographs I have placed on the walls provide the greatest benefit in grieving and remembering. I have one large portrait at the center of the shrine and to the right photographs of my beloved and me together. To the left are photographs of my beloved growing up. Another wall I call the "wall of lasts" contains photographs of the last portrait, last birthday, last Christmas, and other last photos. This is a very intense and sad wall of photographs which both helps me with grieving and reminds me of the love we shared embodied together. The shrine has smaller photographs that were my beloved's favorite photographs which she always kept on the top of her dresser.

Sitting at the shrine provides me with comfort and solace, mixed with sadness and grief. I remember moments captured in the photographs and experience that energy. Of course, it is not necessary to have many photographs displayed. When traveling only one photograph provides an adequate shrine. Surrounding yourself with multiple photographs may not be your preference or provide comfort and solace. As the **I Ching** advises no harm – no blame.

Should you not already have photographs as part of your shrine, consider adding at least your favorite or a few favorites. Add as many photographs as you wish to your shrine. Photographs trigger reminders of loss and love. Photographs may assist you in achieving the balance between experiencing loss and love as well as experiencing the awareness of eternal love.

111 Things That Help Grieving: **#37**

Music

Playing special music as you sit at your shrine can provide a measure of comfort. My favorite is the CD **Harp Magic** by Peter Sterling. You can sample his music on his web site HarpMagic.com. I play music along with lighting incense, lighting candles, sharing black water and cognac (on special days), and writing in my journal each evening. **Harp Magic** has a celestial component that vibrates at a high level of positive energy. While I recommend **Harp Magic,** each person needs to select their own music that provides them with positive energy and perhaps awakens or reawakens celestial memories. Of all of the tracks of **Harp Magic** my favorite is "A Love Eternal." I often stop whatever I am doing and remember as the music reminds me of my eternal love. "A Love Eternal" expands my perspective reminding me that I can see with eyes of love in addition to eyes of loss.

I also recommend **Tao of Healing** and **Tao of Peace** by Dean Evenson and Li Xiangting (Soundings of the Planet).

In addition to playing music at my ceremonies I often sit in silence being open to receive subtle messages and inspiration.

Should you currently not include music as part of your ceremony, consider selecting music that adds positive vibrational energy to your ceremony.

111 Things That Help Grieving: **#38**

Memorials

One of the ways to honor your disembodied loved one is to establish a memorial or memorials. A memorial can be as elaborate as funds to provide training and education or as simple as a black marble urn at your shrine. Memorials include memorial services, obituaries, a CD of photos of your loved one's life to share with family and friends, establishing a shrine, volunteering for a cause or creating a cause, planting trees, honoring last wishes and last requests. The ways to honor your disembodied loved one are limited only by your imagination and resources.

During the last year she was embodied, we took walks in a local botanical garden. On one walk, while looking at the memorial flagstone path with memorial messages carved on many of the stones, Carol Susan announced that she would like a flagstone placed in the garden in her memory. Through my tears and with difficulty speaking I agreed. I am not really sure Carol Susan was all that intent on having a flagstone memorial but I know she was preparing me for her disembodiment. Carol Susan completed a document called **Five Wishes*** that serves as a living will providing advanced directives as well as how she wished to be remembered and last wishes/last requests. Completing the **Five Wishes** document was a loving act of kindness that provided her wishes, requests, and preferences in clear language that assisted in honoring her life according to her wishes and requests. During the early days, weeks, and months following her disembodiment, having clear directions and tasks to complete to honor her were some of the few things I could focus on as well as cared to focus on.

In addition to a memorial service which included eulogies by family and friends, we presented her life in pictures with her requested music and distributed copies of the CD to family and friends after the memorial service. Carol Susan had asked that books be donated to the village of her mother and grandmother in their, as well as her, memory. We established a memorial book fund and have provided multiple shipments of books to the village's schools. Our daughter established a memorial website to honor her mother.

Some memorials are elaborate and require financial support, but memorials can be small and not expensive. Many ceremonies provide memorial honoring functions. Memorials can be public shared with family and friends or private. Many ongoing memorials are likely private or shared with only a few family and friends. Observing special days is both a ceremony as well as serving a memorial function.

It has been my experience that both public shared memorial activities, as well as private memorial events, provide a focus for grief and grieving as well as a measure of comfort, solace, and healing. The size, form, or scope of the memorial is not important. Remembering and honoring your disembodied loved one in whatever way is the important part of memorializing their life and sending your love to them in their new form. I place objects on her shrine – a leaf, flower, stone, seashell, and other things to share my experiences and send my love.

***Five Wishes**, Aging With Dignity, 2009, www.agingwithdignity.org

111 Things That Help Grieving: **#39**

Wearing Black

For the first year of my bereavement I wore black – only black – everything black. Sometime during the second year I added a few purple shirts but still wore mostly black. The third year I added a few purple shirts but still wore mostly black. At the time of this writing at four and one half years I continue to wear mostly black with a few purple shirts. The vibrations of the color black match my own vibrations better than any other color. In some traditions, black is the sign of mourning and therefore a way to "honor the dead" providing unspoken communication to others of the state of mourning. The tradition of wearing black provides me with small comfort as well as honoring my disembodied beloved.

I expanded my wearing black to include items used in my house including black tablecloths, kitchen towels, bathroom towels and mats, bed sheets and covers, and other items. For the first year I burned only black candles. The second year I added a purple candle. Early in the first year, I discovered black water which I added to my ceremonies.

I am not recommending following my tradition of wearing only black the first year and mostly black into the unforeseeable future; however, I encourage you to consider selecting a way to "wear your grief" thereby "honoring your dead." It can be a black arm band or some object used by your disembodied loved one. The concept and practice of wearing your grief does not need to be visible to others unless you so desire. Honoring the dead (or as I prefer to say honoring your disembodied loved one) by wearing black or some other way of wearing your grief is a way of celebrating the life shared together with your beloved in the physical realm and sending love to them in their new form.

I am aware that my embracing the color black may seem excessive and over the top to some. I gain some small measure of comfort surrounding myself in the color that matches the vibrations of my heart. I decided to "scourge my heart out with honest sorrow" and indulge myself with whatever helps to assist me during my experiences in the hellfires of grief.

Should you find this "thing that helps grieving" excessive you can follow the wisdom of the **I Ching** and simply disregard this suggestion. There will be no harm and no blame. On the other hand your embodied soul will rejoice if you find your own ways to "honor the dead" and "the dead" will be thankful you are sending them your love.

Dion Fortune on black:
"The wearing of deep mourning has a very marked psychic effect. Black insulates the wearer from etheric vibrations, and a person so clad is more readily able to get in touch with the subtler planes that one clad in colours, which each attract their corresponding vibrations."*

---

*Dion Fortune. **Dion Fortune's Book of the Dead.** Weiser Books, 2005. First published in 1930 as **Through the Gates of Death**, pages 35-36.

111 Things That Help Grieving: **#40**

Planting A Tree

Planting a tree is both a ceremony and a memorial honoring your disembodied loved one. If you do not have a place to plant a tree, consider asking the locality were you live permission to plant a tree in a park or other public space. Tom Golden in his book, **Swallowed By A Snake***, describes how he, with family and friends, had a tree planting ceremony in a park near where he lives in honor of his disembodied father.

You can decide if you want to plant an evergreen tree or a deciduous tree. The size of the tree depends upon your economic resources, as well as the physical condition of the planters. I chose to plant a ginkgo tree in my back yard. Ginkgo trees have fan shaped leaves which turn a bright yellow-gold in the fall and in the spring produce lovely light green fan shaped leaves. I chose to plant the ginkgo tree on day one thousand since the disembodiment of my beloved soulmate. Day 1000 coincided with our thirty-six wedding anniversary, so the tree planting ceremony was intensely powerful. The plant nursery delivered the thirteen foot ginkgo tree and carted the tree to the hole I had prepared for the root ball. They left the tree beside the hole and I rolled the root ball into the hole as the tree was much too heavy for me to pick up. I burned incense during the digging and planting process. I call the ginkgo tree I planted the 1000 & 36 tree.

I watched the ginkgo tree carefully over the remainder of the summer applying copious amounts of water. Towards the fall I became distressed that the ginkgo leave were turning tan and brown rather than yellow-gold. It seems I had over-watered the ginkgo tree. I provided the ginkgo tree with positive affirmations and loving energy, hoping it would recover in the spring. I carefully observed the smallest buds forming after the tan and brown leaves fell, so I was hopeful for the tree's recovery. In the spring the ginkgo tree produced light green fan shaped leaves and I was appreciative that my excess watering had not drowned the special tree. That summer I indulged the ginkgo tree with benign neglect, meaning that I did not over-water or obsess about the tree's health.

I have related my experience with the ginkgo tree, as the tree planting ceremony and memorial is not without risk. I still watch over the special 1036 tree more closely than any other plant in my yard. I believe that my excess watering was a subtle message that one can be excessive in either direction – too much or too little – and that the golden mean provides balance and avoids extremes.

You may consider a tree planting ceremony as a memorial to your disembodied love one. You can share the ceremony with family and friends or conduct a private ceremony as I did. If you are unable to plant a tree, you can explore the option of adopting a tree in your community.

*Tom Golden. **Swallowed By A Snake**, Book Reference 5, #98.

111 Things That Help Grieving: **#41**

Using Your Disembodied Loved One's Things

One of the ways to honor your disembodied loved one is to use some of their personal possessions. Depending on your level of rawness, you may or may not find comfort, solace, and healing energy in using your disembodied loved one's things. Should the concept feel uncomfortable, it is not the time to consider using your disembodied loved one's things. I recommend saving some of your loved one's special personal possessions as later in your grief and grieving they may offer a measure of comfort, solace, and healing energy.

I have made use of any number of my beloved's possessions some of which she used for many years. Others I store at her shrine. I know that her special possessions retain the smallest amount of her embodied energy and provide me with a small measure of comfort when I use them. I also find comfort when remembering her using the possessions. Using and treasuring your disembodied loved one's special personal possessions honors them and provides healing energy. I have also gifted some of my disembodied loved ones personal possessions to family and friends so that they may also hold and use her favorite personal possessions. I know from personal communications, that the gifted items belonging to my disembodied loved one are treasured by her family and friends.

In sharing the concept of using some of your disembodied loved ones' personal possessions I hope the concept has positive energy for you. You may consider, when the time is right, gifting some of your loved one's things to family and friends so that they may also experience the positive energy of holding and using something treasured by your disembodied loved one. Should the concept have no appeal or positive energy for you, as the **I Ching** advises, there is no harm and no blame.

111 Things That Help Grieving: #42

Removing Sick Room Things

After my beloved's disembodiment there were sick room things scattered about the house with most concentrated in our bedroom. While I was numb with the reality of her death and in massive denial, I somehow intuited that I needed to remove the sick room things. No longer a house of the dying, it was now a house of the dead and the living. I stuck sick room things in closets, cabinets, drawers, boxes, and the trash. The house was converted from a house of the dying to a house of the dead and the living. I could not have articulated the reason for my urgency at time but knew the tasks needed to be done. Thinking about it later, I determined the sick room things triggered memories of her illness and dying. I did not need reminders as the experience was fresh and raw. Putting away the sick room things helped reduce the triggers of her illness and dying. There were more than enough triggers without the sick room things. The conversion from a house of the dying to a house of the dead was an early way to acknowledge my loss and start the long and painful process of bereavement including honoring the dead and honoring the living.

If you have not already, consider converting your house from a house of the dying to a house of the dead and the living. Removing sick room things helps to reduce the constant reminders of dying so the focus can shift to honoring the dead and the living.

111 Things That Help Grieving: **#43**

Sharing Stories

Sharing stories about your disembodied loved one is a powerful way to honor their memory, acknowledge their legacy, and provide a shared experience of the impact of the person while embodied. Sharing stories may be difficult at first due to the raw intensity of your grief. There is no correct time frame for sharing stories. When you are ready to share stories they will bubble up and you will need to tell them and both feel sad and pleased to be honoring your loved one. Sharing stories includes stories about your shared experience as well as remembering and retelling stories told by your disembodied loved one.

Be aware that not all friends and family will be comfortable sharing stories. It may be too distressing for them and they may need more time to grieve in private before they can share stories. Often when you share stories with family and friends it provides them with permission to share their memories of experiences with your disembodied loved one.

A word of caution about sharing stories, there is no gain to sharing negative information about the disembodied person as it neither honors "the dead" or the living. Should you find yourself in the presence of someone who seems intent upon dishonoring both the dead and the living with negative stories remove yourself to a more positive environment. Should you be unable to leave then tell the person you do not want to hear their negative stories. Should they persist, you may need to take them off of your list of people who honor the dead and honor your grief and grieving. You do not need their negative energy.

Some people feel justified talking negatively about the disembodied, believing they need to assist the grieving person to maintain a realistic image of the disembodied. These are usually the same people who want you to "just get over it and get on with your life." These people are not honoring your grief nor honoring the dead. I recommend extending them compassion; however, doing so removed a suitable distance from them.

May you be able to share loving stories of your disembodied loved one with family and friends. I hope you do not need to cope with someone who dishonors the dead and dishonors your grief and grieving. Should you have the misfortune to encounter such a person, recognize their issues as belonging to them and while extending compassion be able to distance yourself to avoid their negative energy. May you have the good fortune beyond measure of having new stories to share about your experiences with your disembodied loved one in their new form. Of course your embodied loved one had limitations, but if you have experienced your disembodied loved one in their spirit form you realize they are somehow merged with their higher self as golden rainbow energy beings. It is not idealizing or deifying your embodied loved one, it is the reality of your spirit realm experience and the reality of your disembodied loved one in their spirit realm form.

111 Things That Help Grieving: **#44**

Black Bow Door Decoration

In earlier times there was a tradition of placing a black wreath on the front door of the house that had experienced the death of a loved one. The black wreath was a sign to all that the people of the house were grieving their loss. Unfortunately this tradition has faded into obscurity. After the disembodiment of my beloved Carol Susan, I removed the fall wreath from the front door and replaced it with a large black bow. The black bow is my version of the traditional black wreath and marks the house as one where people are grieving and honoring the dead.

Honoring the dead provides benefits to both those left behind as well as to the dead. Continuing the relationship by sending and receiving loving energy, which for the living is mixed with loss, grief, and missing the embodied loved one. Each time I see the black bow on the front door I send loving energy to my disembodied loved one and receive her loving energy in return. I am also reminded of my loss and the reality of my experience.

As of this writing the black bow has been on the front door for four and one half years. I feel no need to replace it. Perhaps eventually I will be inspired to change the black bow but for now it is the best door decoration considering the circumstances.

Perhaps you will find the tradition of marking your house to acknowledge your loss and bereavement a helpful way of honoring the dead. Should you not be inspired by a black bow perhaps a bow of the favorite color of your disembodied love one might feel more appropriate.

111 Things That Help Grieving: **#45**

Journaling

After the disembodiment of my beloved I felt too numb and in shock to express my feelings in any way other than tears. At some point I started to feel a need to write about the reality of my experiences, to express myself in words as well as tears. It seemed to me that my embodied soul was demanding that I translate my tears into words. With tears being the language of my embodied soul and with my broken heart providing an improved level of understanding, I started writing in a journal. After a week or so I realized the journal entries were written to my disembodied companion so I started to write directly to her pouring out my words as well as my tears. The daily journal entries are often intensely dark – black - and filled with despair, longing, and yet they have added a level of comfort and healing energy. I know that my disembodied beloved cannot see the journal entries with her physical realm eyes. I also know that she can read my words with her spirit eyes. The image is her spirit presence looking over my shoulder as I write to her in our journal. She does not always like the words I write but rarely complains. I take the rare complaint very seriously. Some might call the complaints subtle whispers from my conscience but I know the source is from beyond the physical realm. All of the words I have written have helped me a little. My beloved's spirit presence looking over my shoulder reading my tears converted into words provides comfort beyond measure.

The words in my journals are descriptions of the reality of my experience expressed as best as I can. After a year I felt compelled to summarize my translation of my tears into poems. I went back to the first journal and starting extracting my experience and summarizing it in poems. In this way the first portions of **Hellfires of Grief I** were written. Then I continued to generate poems based on my journal entries in real time and the rest of **Hellfires of Grief I** and **Hellfires of Grief II** were generated. Being able to look back over my journals and poems provides a much needed perspective regarding the reality of my experience.

The practice of journaling is part of my daily ceremony of honoring my beloved as I light candles, play my favorite music, light incense, and sit beside the shrine and write in the journal. My daily ceremony is usually late at night, the last thing of the day.

If you have never kept a journal (I never kept a journal until after the loss of my embodied companion), I highly recommend sitting aside some time each day to spend converting your feelings, thoughts, tears, and the reality of your experience into words. If you already keep a journal you can consider writing directly to your disembodied love one expressing your grief, missing, longing, and ongoing love. Journaling brings a powerful healing energy and writing directly to your love one allows you to write about things you never said or did but now wish you had and to ask forgiveness for things you said or did and now wish you did not. Converting tears into words provides an expression of your grief and ongoing love in a private sharing between you and the spirit presence of your disembodied love one. This intense sharing provides the healing energy of love that flows back and forth between you and your disembodied loved one.

111 Things That Help Grieving: **#46**

Dream Journaling

Dreams often fade quickly upon waking. The world of dreams is a chaotic place that does not follow the rules of awake time, logic, or linear time. Since the dream time forgetting mechanisms are much stronger that the dream remembering mechanisms, I recommend keeping a pad of paper and pen near the bed so you can jot down a few key words to describe the images from the dream immediately upon waking. This practice will provide the trigger words that will open the gateway into the dream time memories when awake so the dream images can be recorded in your dream journal.

Why do I recommend keeping a dream journal as one of the things that help? If you are fortunate to be blessed with what I call golden dreams you already understand. The healing energy of golden dreams is one of the most powerful things that help grieving. I call dreams that are visits to the spirit realm with my disembodied beloved golden dreams. Golden dreams are called objective dreams by Marie-Louise von Franz.

"A similar situation arises in the interpretation of those dreams wherein the dead appear to a still-living person....and interpret them as if they referred , on the objective level, to the postmortal life of the dead person (not to the life of the dreamer). I have had myself certain dreams which

Jung interpreted in this way, which at the time was rather astonishing to me. He gave no reason for understanding precisely those dreams on the objective level; he usually interpreted such images on the subjective level, that is to say, as symbols of psychic contents to be found in the dreamer himself."*

Marie-Louise von Franz.

Many dreams are subjective dreams referring to internal psychic elements or components of the dreamer, I call them housekeeping dreams. If you are blessed with golden dreams you will be able to intuit the difference. A golden dream is the experience of transcending the physical realm and visiting the spirit realm. In my experience of bereavement, golden dreams have provided the most powerful healing energy as the veil separating the two realms does not exist in golden dreams. I record all the dreams I remember and study them to intuit their message but golden dreams are often experienced at a level well beyond rational thought or the need to study their meanings. Golden dreams offer the most powerful healing of eternal love providing the experience that our loved ones have changed forms, transcended, and while no longer physically present are only a golden dream away. Unfortunately most dreams are of the housekeeping variety and are often dark. Nightmares provide reminders of the black reality of the loss on the physical realm and serve the role of grounding us to the physical plane. As Jeremy Taylor states in his excellent book on dreams:

"...every dream that a person remembers is a 'best fit' – *the best possible dream* for that person to have had at that particular moment."**

Jeremy Taylor

My experience of dream journaling has been invaluable in providing a contrast between my black waking experience of the intense hellfires of grief and my dream time experience of golden dreams. I reread both my journals and dream journals and have condensed my experiences of both realms into poems (**Hellfires I & II** and **Golden Dreams I & II**). Rereading the golden dreams poems is a wonderful experience as they provide a portal to the spirit realm and experiences beyond words as well as beyond measure. Keeping a dream journal may provide you with a glimpse of the spirit realm visits of your embodied soul while your conscious mind is sleeping.

---

*Marie-Louise von Franz. **On Dreams & Death**. Shambhala, 1987, page xv. Note: An expanded version of the Marie-Louise von Franz quote can be found at book reference 9 (#91, page 233).

Jeremy Taylor. **The Wisdom of Your Dreams: Using Dreams To Tap Into Your Unconscious and Transform Your Life. Jeremy P. Tarcher/Penguin, 2009, page 153.

111 Things That Help Grieving: **#47**

Poems/Poetry

"You have that capacity within you to be the poet to your experience….You have to learn how to 'sum up' your experiences in images that convey your personal truth. I do it by writing books on subjects that I wrestle with personally. Many people write songs, poems, and stories. Some, less obviously, make gardens."*

Thomas Moore

My energy healer offered a class on energy healing in the fall of 2012. She started each class with a poem, shared another poem after the break, and ended each class with a poem. Having not read or written poems for a very long time, I found the poems she selected often touched deep levels of my being. I bought a copy of one of the books she used, **The Rag and Bone Shop of the Heart: A Poetry Anthology: Poems for Men** edited by Robert Bly, James Hillman, and Michael Meade (Harper, 1992). Part way through the book I was inspired to write my own poems. I went through my journals extracting the essence of my experiences converting them into poems. I found writing about the reality of my experiences condensed into poems to be a healing activity. After the first hundred or so poems, I decided to share them resulting in **Hellfires of Grief: Love Poems** consisting of 222 poems covering the first eighteen months of my bereavement. I was next inspired to condense my dreams into poems resulting in **Golden Dreams: Companion to Hellfires of Grief: Love Poems** which consists of 111 dream poems covering the same eighteen months.

I have found the writing of poems and rereading them, particularly the golden dream poems, to be an intense healing experience. I often reread **Golden Dreams I** and **Golden Dreams II** to provide the antidote to my daytime experiences in the hellfires of grief (summarized in **Hellfires I** and **Hellfires II**).

The following poem *Tear's Words* describes my experience writing poems as a healing activity.

Tear's Words

poems
my grief concentrated
what my tears say when I listen
my tears insisted I translate them into
words
inspiration from my soul
soul's blood
been said tears are healing
not said how many
if tears are healing
perhaps tear's words
may be healing too

March 23, 2013
Hellfires I, page 276

The poem *A Few Pitiful Poems* summarizes my experience of the limits of writing poems.

A Few Pitiful Poems

our lives condensed into
a few pitiful poems
many more poems
would be needed
to summarize the
good times
black times

life time of poems
would be needed
even then
pitiful summary
of our lives
our love

memories
filled with love
golden dreams
your spirit presence
comforts sustains

poems of love loss
words blood of grief
worse experience of my life
condensed into
a few pitiful poems

March 22, 2013
Hellfires I, page 269

In late 2013, a friend recommended Donald Hall's book of poems, **Without: Poems** written after the disembodiment of his wife, the poet Jane Kenyon. After reading **Without: Poems**, I wanted to read more about Donald Hall's experiences in the hellfires of grief so I read **The Best Day The Worst Day: Life With Jane Kenyon: A Memoir**. I read other bereavement poetry and was inspired to write *poem & POEM*.

poem & POEM

I create
healing poems
not POEMS
not POETRY
not ART
healing poems
heart's tears
translated into words
best I can
not a POET
wounded being
licking my woundedness
with words

October 9, 2013
Hellfires II, page 122

In **Poetic Medicine: The Healing Act of Poem-Making** by John Fox, a certified poetry therapist, Chapter 6: *"When God Sighs: Making Poems About Loss, Illness, and Death: Writing The Winter Gardens of Grief"* he writes:

"For some, writing during an illness or deep grief may not seem possible. For others, poem-making will feel like a natural and essential part of getting through life's greatest challenges and stresses. It will be different for each of us. If writing is not possible just now, *reading poetry* during difficult times may be a great comfort. People have told me reading poetry was the only thing they could do to make it through the brambles of their grief. A woman told me that only poetry was pure enough to soothe her. Reading poems you enjoy may plant seeds for your own writing with the time is ripe."

page 161

Following the wisdom expressed by John Fox, I encourage you to sample a few books of poetry. There are many books of bereavement poetry. I do not know which will speak to you nor likely will you until you sample several. Perhaps you will be inspired to convert your soul's tears, your heart of heart's tears, into healing words. Should reading grief poetry not provide you with healing energy nor inspire you to create your own poems to paraphrase the **I Ching** there is no harm no blame. Perhaps you will find a measure of comfort in grief memoirs or other grief resources.

---

*Thomas Moore, **Dark Nights of the Soul: A Guide To Finding Your Way Through Life's Ordeals.** Penguin, 2004, page 9.

111 Things That Help Grieving: **#48**

Reading Bereavement Books

An avid reader my interest in reading narrowed to a very laser-like focus to only reading grief and bereavement books after the disembodiment of my beloved soulmate. I started with **A Time To Grieve** by Carol Staudacher which I read in small bites. The book offered me solace, compassion, kindness, and wisdom during the darkest times. I have read it many times and given it to family and friends to offer my support and love knowing it will provide comfort.

After reading **A Time To Grieve** a few times, I started reading grief memoirs and grief self help books. Reading grief memoirs enabled me to share vicariously in the experience of others writing about their loss, grief, and dark night of their soul. Grief memoirs are therapeutic both for the author, who needs to share their story, as well as the reader who may find comfort, solace, and perhaps wisdom in reading about the bereavement of others. I have read many grief memoirs and usually find a few jewels in each one. Some have an underlying theme of "getting on with your life" – which mirrors the culture's conventional wisdom and aversion to death, dying, and grief. The "good" grief memoirs teach by positive examples of things that help grieving while the "bad" grief memoirs provide examples of how "to get on with your life."

I have read many self help bereavement books written both by helping professionals and lay persons. Self help books, like grief memoirs, come in all "shapes and sizes" with the content varying from inspired compassionate wisdom to little more that a rehash of the culture's conventional wisdom and attitudes.

Most bereavement books are written years after the writer's experience of loss. If you are early in your grief know the writer is writing about how they remember they coped during the early days, weeks, months, and years with the advantage of years to blur and soften their memories. Writers who use their journals to refresh their memories may express more of the raw, dark, and heaviness of their early days but years have usually intervened to reduce some of the intensity. Reading grief books I would find myself saying "easy for your to say – you've have ten years to adjust." When I started writing grief poems after about a year into my bereavement, I went back to my journals to recapture my experience of those early days and while the poems are intense, raw, dark, and heavy; they are filtered through at least a year of experience and only simulate the despair of those early days, weeks, and months. I found that an awareness of when the grief books were written provided me with an improved perspective so that I did not become discouraged by the relative "ease" of their descriptions of their bereavement and self help advice.

During the darkest times if you are drawn to seek to learn from the experiences, advice, and wisdom of others; reading can provide a form of healing therapy. Bibliotherapy, both formal and informal, has a long and distinguished history. The books listed and briefly described as things that help grieving are those which have been the most helpful to me. I recommend you select books more by inspiration rather than the recommendation of others. That said, if you have been inspired to read some of the books I recommend then you may find some of the others to also be of value. The brief descriptions are offered to see if your intuition inspires you to read them.

For books as thing that help grieving see #83-#100, pages 213-251.

111 Things That Help Grieving: **#49**

Grief Memoirs, Reading

"...but mainly it is what's become know as a 'grief memoir.' Its points of overlap with similar books lead the reader to a conclusion: Without secular rituals to guide us, such memoirs have become our primers in the logic and ethics of mourning. They are what we turn to when we are not sure where else to turn....We live in a culture so preoccupied with happiness, so instrumental in its attitudes, that we forget grief is not something merely to get over, something over which we 'achieve closure,' but a human undertaking, a slow, sticky process of allowing our love to take another, more remote, shape. In **The Light of the World** Alexander discovers warmth that will remind some readers of the deeper truth of grieving: It is a sign of love."*

Meghan O'Rourke
The New York Time Book Review
April 26, 2015

I present a few examples of grief memoirs so you may be encouraged to read a few of the many grief memoirs available. In my experience, grief memoirs offer the companionship of another person who has experienced the hellfires of grief and has courageously decided to share their experience. Reading grief memoirs enables the reader to vicariously share the grief experience of another. Grief memoirs often trigger memories and emotions which facilitate grieving while offering a measure of comfort and companionship during the dark night of the soul.

An often quoted grief memoir is **A Grief Observed** written by C.S. Lewis (HarperCollins, 1961). In the foreword to **A Grief Observed**, Madeleine L'Engle noted both similarities and differences to her grief after the death of her husband and C.S. Lewis after the death of his wife.

Madeleine L'Engle:

"The death of a beloved is an amputation….Like Lewis, I, too, kept a journal, continuing a habit started when I was eight. It is all right to wallow in one's journal; it is a way of getting rid of self-pity and self-indulgence and self-centeredness. What we work out in our journals we don't take out on family and friends. I am grateful to Lewis for the honesty of his journal of grief, because it makes quite clear that the human being is allowed to grieve, that it is normal, it is right to grieve, and the Christian is not denied this natural response to loss. And Lewis asks questions that we all ask: where do those we love go when they die?...I am grateful, too, to Lewis for having the courage to yell, to doubt, to kick at God with angry violence. This is a part of healthy grief not often encouraged."

pages xii, xiv, and xvi
A Grief Observed**

C.S. Lewis:

"No one ever told me that grief felt so like fear. I am not afraid, but the sensation is like being afraid....There is a sort of invisible blanket between the world and me....And no one ever told me about the laziness of grief. Except at my job...I loathe the slightest effort....Meanwhile, where is God?...But go to Him when your need is desperate, when all other help is vain, and what do you find? A door slammed in your face, and a sound of bolting and double bolting on the inside. After that, silence....Not that I am (I think) in much danger of ceasing to believe in God. The real danger is of coming to believe such dreadful things about Him."

pages 3-6

"I not only live each endless day in grief, but live each day thinking about living each day in grief....By writing it all down (all? – no: one thought in a hundred) I believe I get a little outside it....I see people, as they approach me, trying to make up their minds whether they'll 'say something about it' or not. I hate it if they do, and if they don't."

page 10

"But there are other difficulties. 'Where is she now?'...But I find this question, however important it may be in itself, is not after all very important in relation to grief....But don't come talking to me about the consolations of religion or I shall suspect that you don't understand." pages 14-15

A Grief Observed**

Donald Hall:

Donald Hall is the fourteenth poet laureate of the United States. He wrote **Without: Poems** after the death of his wife, the poet Jane Kenyon. **The Best Day The Worst Day: Life With Jane Kenyon*** is an intense grief memoir in which Donald Hall chronicles their lives together, her illness and disembodiment, and his experiences in bereavement.

"Poetry gives the griever not release from grief but companionship in grief. Poetry embodies the complexity of feelings at their most intense and entangled, and therefore offers (over centuries, or over no time at all) the company of tears."

page 118

"My only distraction during Jane's long illness and the first years of mourning consisted of putting her illness and death, and my grief, into words – in conversations or on the page. When I wrote or talked about leukemia and death it was almost as if I were doing something." page 147
The Best Day The Worst Day: Life With Jane Kenyon**

I cannot recommend a particular grief memoir of the many available as some resonate with me and some do not. May reading grief memoirs and vicariously sharing another person's individual experiences in the hellfires of grief offer some comfort and solace.

*Meghan O'Rourke, "To Have Loved and Lost," **The New York Times Book Review,** April 26, 2015, page 16, in reviewing Elizabeth Alexander's grief memoir **The Light of the World: A Memoir**. Meghan O'Rourke has written a grief memoir: **The Long Goodbye**.

C. S. Lewis, **A Grief Observed copyrighted in 1961 under the pseudonym of N. W. Clerk, in 1996 the copyright was restored to C. S. Lewis Pte. Ltd., published by Harper Collins.

***Donald Hall, **The Best Day The Worst Day: Life with Jane Kenyon**, Houghton Mifflin, 2005.

111 Things That Help Grieving: **#50**

A Meditation To Ease Grief (CD)

Belleruth Naparstek. ***A Meditation To Ease Grief***. Health Journeys, 1992. (CD: 50 minutes, $17.98)

Belleruth Naparstek, LISW, is a psychotherapist and expert in guided imagery, positive affirmations, and facilitation of intuition. ***A Meditation To Ease Grief*** starts with an introduction explaining how to best use the CD to ease grief. The CD then provides a section of guided imagery and one of positive affirmations. After listening to the CD a few times you may chose to skip the introduction. You may also discover that you relate better to one or the other sections (guided imagery or affirmations) or you may benefit equally from both.

I listened to ***A Meditation To Ease Grief*** multiple times each day for the first six months of my bereavement. Often I listened the first thing each morning, around midday, early evening, and at bed time. Belleruth Naparstek's voice was comforting, the music soothing, and her guided imagery provided powerful access to my grief. The affirmation section was also powerful and helpful; however, the guided imagery section provided me with the greatest benefit. I have often thought that the CD was perhaps misnamed as I found it to be meditations to ease grieving. Easing grieving means the CD assisted me in suspending my intense denial and more fully encountering my broken heart and grieving more openly in the safe space of the meditation.

While I have adopted any number of Belleruth Naparstek's terms, I continue to use her term "the reality of your experience" converted to "the reality of my experience" to extend increase compassion to myself in my bereavement.

Somewhere around six months I found myself arguing with Belleruth Naparstek during the meditation. While still having healing impact, my disagreements over semantics of a few of her statements suggested I was ready to move on from the CD. Belleruth Naparstek's guided imagery was a wonderful resource during the raw blackness of the first six months of my grieving. I highly recommend the CD: ***A Meditation To Ease Grief.***

for additional information see: www.healthjourneys.com

111 Things That Help Grieving: **#51**

Projects

I invent projects - things to do to provide myself with a respite from the hellfires of grief. My projects have included planting, building various home improvements that were not really necessary, and any number of other things. I invent projects since I have discovered that at times I need to turn down the intensity of the hellfires of grief. Sometimes the projects work for a while. The intensity returns but the projects provide a break - what I call "grieving on the installment plan." Since I am retired I do not need to force myself to put on my work persona (mask/face) and become distracted with the world of work. So I invent projects in order to distract myself. The projects sometimes move my grief from the foreground to the background while I concentrate on the project. Projects spike in spring and summer as those two seasons have an abundance of special days – birthdays, anniversaries, Mother's day, and memories of vacations past.

For a number of years I felt vaguely guilty for inventing projects. Planting many plants, making unnecessary home improvements – justifying my frenzy of activity by telling myself the improvements increase property value. I knew I was really taking a break from facing loss, death, grief, missing, and being exhausted by the intensity of my grief. Next I told myself the activities were helping me become better grounded and not always trying to see past the veil separating the physical realm from the realm of spirit. I knew I was really taking a break from facing loss, death, grief, missing, and being exhausted by the intensity of my grief. Now at four and a half years, I think the projects are an attempt to achieve improved balance by immersion in physical realm activities - a modest reinvestment in physical realm life. I still find more than enough time to contemplate the mysteries of life and death. I have decided that sometimes it is OK to take a little break. I am grieving on the installment plan because I cannot do it any other way. So inventing projects does not seem quite so negative anymore. Perhaps projects assist me to improve my balance and focus at least for a while on the latest project or projects. Grieving on the installment plan is necessary for me to face the most traumatic experience of my life – the disembodiment of my beloved. I know I am really taking a break from facing loss, death, grief, missing, and being exhausted by the intensity of my grief.

I must confess that I often find myself silently asking Carol Susan how she likes the latest project. Sometimes I hear her subtle whispered response. So projects are not so bad after all.

I hope this thing that helps is of value to you if you find yourself indulging in projects that you have invented. As the **I Ching** advises no harm – no blame. A project or two may assist in establishing balance and bring healing energy.

Section Three

Healing

"I will not expect to heal by running away from conditions, reactions, and emotions that arise as a result of this death. I will not remain passive and assume things will get better. I will put forth effort to make progress through this grieving process. This will include recalling, feeling, sharing, and memorializing my loved one. Today I will do one of those things; tomorrow I will to another. And I will continue on, day after day, until I know in my heart and mind that I have confronted the most difficult part of this sorrow."*

Carol Staudacher

The work of healing after the disembodiment of a loved one is the hardest and most painful work. Not only is grief work necessary for healing but is an ongoing life long process. The old adage that time heals all wounds is not completely true or totally accurate. Without the work of grieving, time stands still along with healing. The complexity of healing involves body, emotion, mind, heart, soul, and spirit. Healing requires attention to all of these.

---

*Carol Staudacher. **A Time To Grieve: Meditations for Healing After the Death of A Loved One.** HarperCollins, 1994, pages 92-93.

111 Things That Help Grieving: **#52**

Healing

For about the first year and a half, I considered healing to be an alien concept. I was too raw, black, and heavy with grief, despair, longing, and wishing to consider the concept of healing to be anything but an attempt to force the idea of healing on me by a death and grief adverse culture. The focus on healing angered me as it seemed to be a not so subtle way of encouraging me to keep my grief to myself, out of sight, and to get on with my life. As the life I had known for thirty-four years had just ended, the idea of healing irritated the hell out of me.

Later thinking about the grief and bereavement books I read during the first several years, I realized the authors were often years beyond the moment of the loss of their loved one. I also began to realize that my primitive, instinctive, and intuitive efforts to cope with the loss of my soulmate were attempts to protect my body, mind, embodied soul, and spirit from the trauma of my loss.

Just managing to hold on by a thread - wondering why? Perhaps wondering why is a form of healing as well. Wondering why the thread still exists may be the way of healing. That only part of my embodied soul accompanied my beloved as she returned to our spirit realm home suggested to me that it was not my time to disembody. I continue to have necessary lessons to learn in the school of embodied life, have not completed the purpose(s) of this incarnation, and have not completed the life tasks I signed up to complete. Of course, this is conjecture as I do not remember any such pre-embodied agreements. I do get glimpses or hints from time to time in my dreams and in other ways.

The concept of grief as a healing journey was even more absurd to me and continues to irritate the hell out of me. There may be some parallels to the hero's journey but only if the "hero" is severely wounded and hanging on by a thread. The night sea journey in a flimsy boat with minimal power, the underground journey into the hellfires of grief, and getting lost in the primordial forest of grief are all images of a person heart wounded by loss and struggling to maintain the bare minimum of balance or equilibrium.

For years I have wondered what healing looks like and have developed a number of ideas, none of which provide much, if any, solace to my grieving heart. Perhaps healing is achieving some form of equilibrium or balance after the trauma of loss. Balance after loss is difficult to achieve as the balance of old no longer works. Of the numerous ways I have endeavored to understand healing perhaps the most helpful as been the concept that healing is a striving to obtain a balance between the realities of my two realms of experience. In the physical realm loss prevails while in the spirit realm love prevails. Healing seems to be a balance of the two realms of experience - holding both loss and love simultaneously. I rarely achieve the still point between the two realities of experience. Achieving balance often seems more of a theoretical concept than a practical experience.

One concept that does not work, in spite of conventional wisdom, is that the simple passage of time will heal. With the passage of time one may become more accustomed to the woundedness of loss, more resigned to the ugly reality of loss and a broken heart, and more accustomed to the empty place once filled by the physical presence of one's beloved. To me this does not feel like healing. For me healing is experiencing physical realm loss blended with the experience of spirit realm love.

I have used the word "healing" rather than the word "healed" as I know healing to be a lifelong process. I do know what healing looks like as I experience being healed in golden dreams. Then I awake from the dream into the reality of my experience as a wounded survivor. Golden dreams provide powerful healing experiences as they provide golden energy to balance the black hellfires of grief.

111 Things That Help Grieving: **#53**

Golden Dreams

Golden dreams are dreams in which my dream body travels beyond the physical realm to the spirit realm where I visit with my beloved in an aspect of her spirit form, as well as with an aspect of my higher self and others. Contrary to some dream interpretations not all dreams are wish fulfillment or subjective projections of aspects of one's self. Some dreams are as C.G. Jung and Marie-Louise von Franz termed "objective dreams." My dream visits with my beloved are summarized in **Golden Dreams I** and **Golden Dreams II** which are collections of my dreams after the disembodiment of my beloved summarized in free form poems. While some might call these dreams metaphysical or transpersonal, I prefer to call them golden dreams due to the golden energy that surrounds the images in the dream and the golden energy of remembering some of golden dreams upon waking. Golden dreams have provided the most powerful healing energy during my four and one half years of bereavement.

May sharing my golden dreams and the concept of golden dreams remind you of your dream visits to the spirit realm and meetings with your loved ones. Should you not remember golden dreams and therefore believe you have not experienced travel to the subtle spirit realm in your dreaming body, may you be blessed with often remembering your experience of golden dreams. Golden dreams provide a glimpse of the sacred spirit realm and our spirit realm home. Of all the things that have helped grieving, remembering golden dreams has been one of the most powerful as they facilitate the transformation of the physical realm relationship to a spirit realm relationship. Golden dreams do not remove the reality of my experience of the loss of my embodied soulmate. Golden dreams do provide an expanded reality of my experience of the eternal love of the spirit realm.

Note: For additional information about objective dreams see Marie-Louise von Franz, **On Dreams and Death: A Jungian Interpretation**. Book Resource 9, Thing That Helps Grieving #91, page 233.

111 Things That Help Grieving: **#54**

Messages

"It isn't a question, anyway, of deciding whether we should or should not give attention to the dead. They present themselves to us in unsought memories, in dreams, and in momentary visitations during the day or night…"*

                                                Thomas Moore

James Van Praagh in his book **Heaven and Earth: Making the Psychic Connection** (2001) Chapter Four: "Signals From Spirit: Various Methods Spirits Use to Contact Us" describes both mental and physical phenomena used by spirits for contacting the physical realm. Mental phenomena include dreams, inspirations, and automatic writing. Physical phenomena include temperature change, electrical occurrences, rapping and knocking, electric voice, spirit lights, telephone and television communications, apparitions, materializations, spirit photography, trance medium ship, transfiguration, and apports. Van Praagh also discusses clairvoyance and clairaudience as well as smell, touch, and taste.

My most powerful messages have usually been delivered in golden dreams. There have been numerous other forms of communication as well. Infrequently, but with intense impact, I hear Carol Susan's voice providing me with a message wrapped in loving energy beyond words. I often receive inspirations and encouragement both from

Carol Susan and other spirit realm helpers. There have been many other types of messages covering most of the categories described by James Van Praagh.

Christmas Card 2011 is one example. Carol Susan disembodied to return to our spirit realm home on October 31, 2011. A week or so before Christmas Day, I received a card from one of her colleague-friends containing a second card. Carol Susan had given her some books when we were moving and later when she picked up one of the books a card fell out. The card was a Christmas card Carol Susan was planning to give me that had been lost in all of the chaos of her illness and our moving. The card was one of the Boynton cat cards we have been giving one another for over 34 years – often the same one. The very first awful Christmas without Carol Susan in her embodied form she sent me a very special Christmas card. I held her card both crying and feeling our loving connections across the realms.

James Van Praagh has written at least eight books about his work as a medium starting with **Talking To Heaven: A Medium's Message of Life After Death** (1997). If you have not discovered James Van Praagh's books, I highly recommend them. Reading them in the order written is also recommended as Van Praagh shares his learning from his contacts with spirits as his work progresses.

Another medium to consider, if you have not discovered him, is George Anderson. George Anderson has written three books with Andrew Barone: **Lessons from the Light** (2000), **Walking in the Garden of Souls** (2001), and **What Souls in the Hereafter Can Teach Us About Life** (2012). Joel Martin and Patricia Romanowski have published a series of conversations with George Anderson including **We Don't Die** (1988), **We Are Not Forgotten** (1991), and **Our Children Forever** (1994).

---

*Thomas Moore, **Soul Mates: Honoring the Mysteries of Love and Relationship**. 1994, page 203.

111 Things That Help Grieving: **#55**

Inspirations

The disembodiment of a loved one is a heart breaking, world altering experience. A broken heart is a raw, wounded, and open heart. Having an open heart is also referred to as being soft hearted. The heart during the experience of loss is well beyond soft as the heart feels severely wounded, fragmented, and raw.

One's heart opens in a spiral progression which may be very rapid with the trauma of loss. Within the heart exists one's heart of hearts which is the realm of the embodied soul. With the loss of your beloved you can expect to receive messages and assistance from your helpers. Helpers take many forms including guardian angels, ancestors, power animals, the spirit form of your beloved, and others. Inspirations may come in dreams - golden, black, and others; subtle whispers, and urgings from unknown sources. I was inspired to start writing about my experiences of loss, grief, and grieving in a journal. I was also inspired to start a dream journal so I could focus on my dreaming life as well as my waking life. I was inspired to create a shrine to honor my disembodied beloved, to wear black, and many of the other activities that I have written about as things that help grieving. The decision to condense my journals writings into poems was another inspiration. This book was inspired and encouraged by dreams and other subtle messages.

The importance of messages and inspirations regarding loss, grief, and grieving is the profound wisdom beyond what is routinely available in the physical realm. Inspirations are provided by spirit realm helpers including your higher self, the higher self of your beloved, your ancestors, guardian angels, and higher energy beings beyond my ability to describe. Being broken hearted by your loss, while an intensely painful experience and the most awful experience of your embodied existence, provides the opening for your embodied soul to also whisper to you along with all of your other helpers. Successful grief work is being open to these inspirations and acting on them as they provide powerful healing energies. This is not to suggest that the grieving process will be expedited or speeded up by being open to these messages. Embracing grief and grieving with an open heart is ugly, painful work. Purifying the dark parts of yourself and eventually discovering your golden essential nature requires courage, perseverance, and the ability to remain open hearted in a culture that reinforces being hard hearted, aggressive, and competitive. These values encourage people to close and harden their hearts, to "just get over it," and "just get on with your life" which reinforces pushing grief underground where it often creates additional problems. Neglecting, ridiculing, or ignoring messages and inspirations is not the way of courageous grieving. Being open to messages and inspirations helps weaken the veil separating the physical and spirit realms. With good fortune beyond measure as the messages and inspirations continue, the separation becomes less defined and ultimately disappears. This is speculation on my part as my experience has not progressed to such a level of permeability.

It is worth mentioning that messages and inspirations may take the form of embodied persons who are either channels for subtle spirit realm wisdom or are some form of earth angel or other healing energy.

As healing progresses, you may experience your heart as less raw and wounded; however, healing does not produce a hard heart armored against the pain of loss but an open heart able to receive the messages, inspirations, and love from both the physical and spirit realms.

111 Things That Help Grieving: **#56**

Making Room

The inspiration for the concept of making room came from a dream. In the dream I am visiting the spirit realm and a spirit realm energy being I knew was my beloved Carol Susan. Carol Susan told me that I needed to make more room for the spirit realm Carol Susan. The message was given with what I can only describe as pure golden love. Upon awakening I have treasured this golden dream, often pondered it, and written about it often. At one level I immediately understood the message to mean that I needed to spend less time remembering, reminiscing, and looking back over our embodied lives together. My focus on the disembodied physical Carol Susan has consumed much of my time and energy.

Making room for the spirit realm Carol Susan means understanding that she has changed forms and that I need to look forward into the spirit realm to continue our experiences together with the level of intensity deserving of soulmates now spiritmates or more accurately, since I am still embodied, a mixture of soulmatespiritmates. I often pause to evaluate how I am progressing in making more room for the spirit realm and usually determine I continue to come up short. I do experience wonderful visits to the spirit realm and remember some of them in golden dreams. I am open to receive subtle messages, inspirations, and other forms of communication from the spirit realm. While I continue to look back experiencing the heartbreaking sadness of the disembodiment of my soulmate, I have made some room for the spirit realm.

I cannot clearly explain why I have not made more room for the spirit realm and the spirit realm form of my soulmate. I can only speculate that I have more time to spend sitting in the hellfires of grief and burning away more of my imperfections. I treasure memories of my embodied soulmate and hold them in my heart of hearts. I have no intention of letting them go. Perhaps making room suggests achieving more of a balance than I currently experience. I suspect looking back and remembering the loving shared memories is not part of the making more room recommendation. I intuit that spending less time on regrets and remorse for errors of omission and errors of commission would provide more than enough room to experience the spirit realm more fully. I am making slow progress. At this time it is the best I can do within my limitations. It will have to be good enough for now.

Perhaps the concept of making room will provide you with a way to consider how to both maintain, as well, as enhance your ongoing experiences with your disembodied loved one. May you be open to the subtle messages from your disembodied loved ones as well as others so that they can provide you with ongoing love, guidance, and healing energy.

111 Things That Help Grieving: **#57**

Forgiveness

"The biggest part of it is about forgiveness."*
Carol Susan DeVaney-Wong

During the blackest times after Carol Susan disembodied, as part of my grieving, I was conducting a life review. My life review consisted mostly of considering all of my errors of omission and errors of commission – things I did not say or did not do that I wished I had and things I did say or do that I wished that I had not. I was recycling the errors, real and imagined over and over when Carol Susan said, "The biggest part of it is about forgiveness." Her words were accompanied by love, compassion, and acceptance. Beyond the words were other gifts beyond description. I immediately wrote down her words and reflect on them when I find myself being overly critical. Forgiveness of oneself is easy to say, but true forgiveness is at the level of the heart. The head makes excuses – I am only a flawed human so what can you expect – however real forgiveness requires looking at the dark side of one's self and not only acknowledging the "monsters" but transforming them into positive aspects and positive energy. Converting the alchemical lead into celestial gold. I continue to look back some times with regrets and remorse. More often I look back with gratitude and appreciation for the experiences we shared embodied together. I am now more focused on new shared experiences in a more complex relationship than the one we shared embodied together. So little by little I am sneaking up on forgiveness, one negative at a time, slowly converting and channeling energy in more positive ways.

May you find forgiveness at the level of your heart for any and all of your short comings, real and imagined. The loss of a loved one creates a black time when the life review is conducted in the hellfires of grief often with little compassion, loving kindness or forgiveness. May you experience the ongoing love, compassion, and acceptance from your disembodied loved one and that you can experience the state beyond forgiveness.

*Carol Susan DeVaney-Wong personal communication

111 Things That Help Grieving: **#58**

Within My Limitations

I have adopted the phrase "I am doing the best I can within my limitations" from Carol Susan. I often add the phrase "and that will have to be good enough" and sometimes add "for now" to provide room for improvement. The phrase supports being gentle and treating oneself with loving kindness during the black days of grief and grieving. It is a wonderful experience to receive love, support, comfort, encouragement, and other forms of positive regard from family and friends. It can be undone if you do not also embrace the support and add your own self love, support, comfort, encouragement, and other forms of positive regard to yourself.

There are times when "doing the best that I can within my limitations" does not seem to be good enough. During these times I indulge myself with fault finding recounting my regrets at my errors of commission and errors of omission. Perhaps the standard I compare myself to is unrealistic, as well as unobtainable, given my current limitations. My higher self, whom I occasionally glimpse, is certainly well beyond my current level of functioning. Brief glimpses of my higher self provide me with a goal or standard to strive to emulate. I am aware this is an unrealistic expectation as my focus is on regaining my equilibrium from the trauma of the disembodiment of my soulmate. During these moments of reflection the phrase I adopted from Carol Susan proves most helpful. As a wounded embodied soul experiencing the hellfires of grief and black nights of the soul, hearing myself repeat Carol Susan's phrase provides a healing moment and serves a healing function. I can then acknowledge that yes, I am doing as well as I can within my limitations and that is good enough for now.

Sometimes if I am quiet enough the phrase seems to be spoken in a subtle whisper by my embodied soul and at other times by my disembodied beloved. I hope in your quiet moments you can hear your soul's subtle voice whispering, as well as that of your disembodied loved one.

111 Things That Help Grieving: **#59**

Eyes of Love/Eyes of Loss

After the disembodiment of my beloved my vision was limited to seeing almost everything through eyes of loss. My vision was limited to my loss with almost everything being viewed through the lens of that loss. At the very first, I was functioning on some kind of automatic remote control with denial and dissociation from my emotions being my way of coping. Of course my grief broke through often and with intensity. Looking with eyes of loss, I mainly saw the black dragon named grief. Perhaps I was looking through the dragon's eyes. My world became black as if it was always night no matter the time. The only bright spots were family and friends who were also suffering their own black nights of the soul. Looking through eyes of loss it is very difficult to count your blessings or recognize your good fortune to have experienced the physical presence and love of your loved one for however long (34 years with my beloved).

Everything I saw reminded me of my loss. Little things, big things, her bar of soap in the shower, our special little spoon, her car, our house we picked out and fixed up together, and many others – almost anything and everything. The first golden dream, when Carol Susan appeared in her angel/goddess form was such an intense experience – bathed in her golden radiant love I was able to look through eyes of love at least while experiencing and remembering the dream. Over time golden dreams and other subtle messages allowed me to see from eyes of love more often. One day I realized I had reached a balance between the two ways of seeing when I was able to both experience my intense grief at my loss while at the same moment holding my experience of loving and being loved. I was then able to both count my blessings as well as count my losses.

The image of seeing with eyes of loss and eyes of love enabled me to recognize which set of eyes I was using – usually not a difficult determination – and to slowly see with eyes of love more frequently. For the first two plus years, eyes of loss prevailed. As of this current moment (four and one-half years) while writing about the two kinds of seeing eyes of loss continue to prevail.

After I started thinking about which types of eyes I was using, I was often able to identify my seeing only with eyes of loss and open my heart to experience eyes of love. When all else fails to shift my vision, remembering golden dreams helps me reconnect to seeing with eyes of love. Rereading golden dreams helps shift my way of seeing to eyes of love reminding me of being blessed with eternal love.

111 Things That Help Grieving: **#60**

**Possession in Great Measure/
Possession Beyond Measure**

Should you be fortunate enough to have members of your soul group as family and/or friends you know the experience of possession in great measure. If you have been most fortunate to discover your soulmate in this incarnation, you are clearly blessed and know the experience of possession in great measure. Of course, the possession is love. When you lose family and friends the possession in great measure turns to the dark side and you experience loss and grief in equal measure to the love shared. Possession of love in great measure when loss occurs turns to possession of grief in great measure. I do not know how it could be any other way.

If you are fortunate to continue your relationship with your disembodied family and friends, you are blessed with possession beyond measure. Should your soulmate be the one who has disembodied, your loss and grief may well seem beyond measure. If you are blessed with golden dreams and other messages from your disembodied loved ones, you know the experience of possession beyond measure. The possession is, of course, eternal love.

The most healing experiences during my bereavement (four and one half years at this writing) have been my experiences of golden dreams, subtle whispers, and the spirit presence of my beloved. The experience of her looking over my shoulder as I write to her in my journal is a feeling of everlasting love. Many of my ceremonies and activities send my love and appreciation to my disembodied friends and family, especially to my beloved soulmate.

May the language of possession in great measure and possession beyond measure provide you with a vision of love beyond your loss and grief. The experiences of eternal love does not eliminate loss and grief as the formerly embodied loved one continues to be disembodied; however, I would not wish to experience the dark side of possession in great measure without the healing energy of possession of eternal love beyond measure. I end each of my journal entries with "I love you always forever and beyond." May you be blessed with possession in great measure **and** possession beyond measure.

Note: My use of the language of "possession in great measure" is taken from the I Ching.

111 Things That Help Grieving: **#61**

Kindness

Carol Susan promoted the practice of doing at least one act of loving kindness every day. She said that if everyone did at least one act of loving kindness every day the world would be a much better place. She did not keep count of her acts of loving kindness as they seemed a natural part of her being. Watching her interact, often with total strangers, I was always amazed by how effortless her acts of loving kindness seemed.

Since her disembodiment, I have made a conscious effort to emulate her, to the best of my ability, as well as honoring her by doing at least one act of loving kindness each day. Often the person most in need of acts of loving kindness is the person grieving the loss of their loved one. When I find myself indulging in personal fault finding, regrets, or other negative thinking directed towards myself, I quite often hear Carol Susan tell me that I am doing the best that I can within my limitations and that it is good enough. I am always heartened by these subtle messages and realize her acts of loving kindness have transcended her disembodiment.

Providing at least one act of loving kindness towards others while grieving acknowledges that the loss of your loved one is also a loss of that same person for others, perhaps many others. Many of the things that help my grieving involving my disembodied loved one also have provided a small amount of loving kindness towards others who are also grieving the loss of their family member, friend, colleague, and/or mentor.

Acts of loving kindness do not need to be big or flashy nor are they offered with strings attached or the expectation of reciprocity. Acts of loving kindness are food for the soul, both the souls of others as well as your own. Simple acts of support and encouragement can have a large impact. Many people already have their own internal critic and do not need an external one to reinforce their already more than adequate internal critic. An act of loving kindness is to resist the temptation to offer criticism to others, no matter how well intended you think it to be, particularly during periods of intense grieving. The same advice holds true directed towards one's self. If you are grieving and others are not making an effort to offer you support, comfort, and solace, in whatever form they can, then they are not practicing loving kindness. These folk are dealing with their own pathology relating to dying, death, and mortality and your grief is disturbing their pathological denial. If at all possible extend yourself an act of loving kindness and stay as far away from them as possible. If for whatever reason you cannot avoid them, make every effort to discount their negative acts of unkindness.

May you find the concept of acts of loving kindness of value in your struggles with the loss of your loved one. May you be surrounded by others who provide you with acts of loving kindness during your black nights of the soul. May you be able to extend acts of loving kindness towards yourself during the black times when a small act of kindness provides huge benefits for your grieving heart and embodied soul.

May you be able to recognize those who, for whatever reason, are unable to be supportive and take distance from them either physical distance and/or emotional distance.

111 Things That Help Grieving: **#62**

Courage To Grieve

It may appear self evident that grieving is one of the things that helps grieving. It is usually not possible to fully turn off grief and grieving. Grief and grieving happen. Even if you are usually able to suppress mourning, the public display of bereavement, grief builds up and leaks out even when you are trying to contain your grief. Having the courage to grieve acknowledges that grieving is intensely painful hard work. The loss of a loved one creates a huge empty place in your world and an equally huge empty place in your broken heart. Giving yourself permission to grieve means encountering your loss as directly as possible and not employing excessive coping strategies to suppress and avoid your grief. There are many ways to attempt to avoid grief. Excessive sleep, excessive alcohol consumption, excessive use of drugs, keeping constantly busy to avoid facing the loss, excessive television, excessive internet or gaming activity, and other avoidance strategies that attempt to reinforce the denial of loss and death.

Grieving requires courage to face the reality of the experience of loss and the intense emotions generated by the disembodiment of a loved one. Grieving is a raw, dark, and heavy experience that requires courage to face directly. The loss of a loved one is a traumatic life experience and depending on the relationship may be **the** most traumatic experience of a life time. As if the loss of a loved one is not traumatic enough, many discover grief is accompanied by other dark experiences. The loss of a loved one brings us face to face with the reality of death. Fear of death and dying is epidemic in many cultures and reminders of the reality of death and dying are strongly discouraged. So in addition to the trauma of loss of a loved one is the culture's negative attitude about mourning, grief, and grieving. The personal denial of the painful reality of loss, which is usually only partially successful, is significantly rewarded and reinforced by the culture.

Courage is required to directly encounter your loss and give yourself permission to grieve. Courage is also required to grieve in spite of the many messages from the culture to "just get over it and get on with your life" or some variation of the theme. The courage to grieve requires an open heart so you can follow the subtle whispers of your heart of hearts, your embodied soul. Allowing yourself to drop into the dark night of the soul, experience the hellfires of grief, and slowly start the hero's journey to travel beyond the physical realm of loss until you experience the spirit realm of eternal love. Not a quick or easy quest to take the night sea journey to confront your demons and learn to transform your vision from eyes of loss to eye of love.

You can expect only others who have faced their experience of loss and given themselves permission to grieve will honor your grief and appreciate your courage. Others will avoid you to avoid the reality of death and dying.

May you face the traumatic loss of your loved one with courage to honor them as well as your embodied soul by giving yourself permission to grieve. Providing yourself with permission to grieve in whatever way seems appropriate to you is the courageous act of a hero (heroine) who rather than riding on the tail of the dragon named grief being whipped about while attempting to deny the experience to riding at the head of the dragon to jumping into the mouth of the dragon named grief to be transformed by the experience.

Note: see naming grief, #24, page 70.

111 Things That Help Grieving: **#63**

Animal Companion

If you already have an animal companion you can skip this thing that helps grieving as you are already experiencing the benefits of sharing your life with your animal companion.

Having an animal companion to care for and love and receiving their love in return assists in grounding, as well as reaffirming the simple pleasures of physical realm life during a time when the dark side clouds almost everything. When you live alone having an animal companion is particularly beneficial as sharing your life with your animal companion provides healing energy and their physical presence companionship.

At this point in this thing that helps I need to make the disclaimer that I am a "cat person" so if you are a "dog person" you need to translate my cat preference to your dog preference.

I was staying with my daughter in late 2012 when she decided she wanted two kittens. She located two and we went to visit. When the breeder brought the two kittens to my daughter their mother, Lauren, followed. She climbed onto the back of my chair and proceeded to "groom" my hair. The breeder was surprised as Lauren had not approached other people much less "groomed" them. A month later when we returned to pick up the two kittens, I told the breeder I would be pleased to adopt Lauren when she was ready to retire. She agreed. We left with two very small fur balls. I found watching the two little kittens exploring, playing, and sleeping on my lap to be a comfort during my dark times. My grief counselor said they were two little healers. She was absolutely correct. Holding a tiny kitten in my hand and listening to the kitten's baby purring is a healing experience. Watching the two kittens playing reawakened my sense of pleasure in the simple things of life which I was convinced had departed permanently.

In early 2014 Lauren retired and I adopted her after she had already selected me in October 2012. Of course I spoil her outrageously. She climbs onto my lap and then onto my chest with her head under my chin or on my shoulder. I hold her and rub her while she purrs. She decides to lick me from time to time as well. Lauren is a wonderful healing presence as my animal companion.

If you do not have an animal companion, consider adopting an animal companion of your preference, particularly if you live alone. There are many benefits to having an animal companion. Animal companions are natural healers, provide unconditional love, and are excellent teachers at being in the moment. My daughter's two kittens and their mother, Lauren, have assisted me in rediscovering a few of life's simple pleasures coexisting with the hellfires of grief.

111 Things That Help Grieving: **#64**

Compassion

Conventional wisdom maintains that grief and grieving are self-indulgent and selfish. I offer the word "compassionate" as a better choice of words. Experiencing a heart breaking loss alters the reality of experience. Adrift in the night sea journey on an angry sea, descending into the hellfires of grief, and experiencing the black nights of the soul demands a major shift in energy. When hanging on by a thread, raw, heavy, and dark with despair pulling in your energy to lick your woundedness and grieve your loss is self-indulgent and selfish. It is also an essential self protective act of loving kindness towards your self. Extending compassion towards your self is one of the keys to coping with the complicated landscape of loss and grief. Perhaps the best advice one is offered during the darkest of times – perhaps inspired by your embodied soul and your spirit realm helpers – is to be gentle, kind and loving towards yourself and your embodied loved ones also left behind and suffering.

An excellent resource on selfishness is the book written in 1937 by David Seabury **The Art of Selfishness**. The opposite of selfish is selfless so the golden mean is a balance of the two. Telling someone they are being selfish is often a manipulative ploy to force them to change usually towards the accuser preferences.

If someone suggests your grief and grieving is self-indulgent and/or selfish, consider this to be a positive affirmation that you are extending loving kindness and compassion towards yourself. Being gentle with oneself and your embodied loved ones provides much needed support and establishes a foundation for self-forgiveness for real and/or imagined errors of omission and commission that will likely plague you during your bereavement.

Note: The book **The Art of Selfishness** has been reprinted multiple times and continues to be available.

111 Things That Help Grieving: **#65**

Enough

"I wish you enough sun to keep your attitude bright.
I wish you enough rain to appreciate the sun more.
I wish you enough happiness to keep your spirit alive.
I wish you enough pain so that the smallest joys in life appear much bigger.
I wish you enough gain to satisfy your wanting.
I wish you enough loss to appreciate all that you possess.
I wish you enough 'Hello's' to get you though the final 'Good-bye.'"*

Bob Perks

Carol Susan liked the wishes and the story that went with the wishes. She gave me a copy of the story and wishes in the last year of her embodied life. I must confess that I did not then nor do I now have anything approaching Carol Susan's equanimity. I contemplate "enough" regularly, generalizing "enough" to include my resilience, coping, and adjusting being "enough," Often none of this seems like "enough." As Carol Susan would say I am doing the best I can within my limitations. It will have to be good "enough." Sometimes it almost is. As for the "final" good-bye, I do not believe the "final" good-bye is "final" as I experience golden dreams and eternal love.

You can read the full story of "I Wish You Enough Love" at Bob Perks web site (www.IWishYouEnough.com).

I wish enough love for all. I further wish our equanimity to be enough to endure the "final" physical realm good-bye and that we are all blessed with golden dreams in abundance and eternal love.

---

*Bob Perks, "I Wish You Enough," in Jack Canfield and Mark Victor Hansen. **Chicken Soup for the Grieving Soul: Stories About Life, Death and Overcoming the Loss of a Loved One.** Chicken Soup for the Soul Publishing, 2012, page 188.

111 Things That Help Grieving: **#66**

Achieving Balance

For years I thought balance was achieved by looking with eyes of love equally with eyes of loss. I now consider this an early level or stage of balance. Balance between honoring the dead and honoring the living is another, perhaps higher, level of balance. The concept of achieving balance has developed and evolved during four and one half years of bereavement. Achieving balance honoring the dead equally with honoring the living is a work in progress. Balance at another level is making room for the spirit realm while not losing one's grounding in the physical realm.

Achieving balance is not easily accomplished. Achieving balance is a lifelong process with moments of balance or equilibrium alternating with moments of imbalance or disequilibrium. Often in the early years grief, bereavement, and loss prevail. With the experience of golden dreams and other inspirations, I started to consider my blessings – my good fortune in great measure. Gratitude and appreciation for my experience of finding my soulmate and spending years embodied together enabled me to slowly balance the experience of loss with the experience of love. Balance is a delicate condition, as simple experiences can prove disruptive. A shared favorite song, memory, photograph, holiday, anniversary, birthday, and other experiences create the conditions that favor seeing with eyes of loss rather than eyes of love.

In my experience, during the early days following loss moments focused on love, gratitude, and appreciation were less frequent and intensely treasured. The process of achieving balance is neither linear nor permanent. Achieving balance is a dynamic process often with the experience of more imbalance than balance.

Do not become discouraged with the difficulties obtaining and maintaining balance. Grief and grieving is a lifelong experience. The form and intensity may change over time, particularly if you have the good fortune beyond measure of experiencing golden dreams, other inspirations, and messages from the spirit realm.

111 Things That Help Grieving: **#67**

Sharing Quintessence: Alchemy

In the alchemical literature beyond the four elements of the physical realm (earth, air, fire, water) exists a fifth element called by many names with "quintessence" being one of the most frequent names used. Essence is focused on characteristics within the physical realm available to the physical senses (often enhanced by technology). Quintessence is both above and below and is equally present in the physical realm and spirit realm. It may be considered the life force, spirit energy, embodied soul, heart of hearts, and many other names. Quintessence is invisible to the physical senses, being observed only by metasenses which are within the domain of the embodied soul.
The quintessence is the essence of the essence. Quintessence is subtle, incorruptible, and celestial in nature.

Sharing quintessence is an important part of many wisdom traditions. The ceremony of setting a place at the table for the disembodied loved one is a common practice in some cultures. Setting out food and drink for the ancestors, gods and goddesses, and others is an important part of many ceremonies. Sharing quintessence is one way of honoring the dead. "The dead" are not dead but transformed into their quintessence; therefore, my use of the term "disembodied" honors the quintessence of my loved one who has left the physical realm to return to our spirit realm home. Sharing quintessence also honors your embodied soul as well as your spirit realm helpers.

In burning incense the essence of the incense – smoke, fragrance, ashes – remain within the physical realm: however, the quintessence of the incense transcends the physical realm to be experienced in the spirit realm. Lighting candles also has both essence energy and quintessence energy. Many of my ceremonies involve sharing quintessence with my beloved and others. In addition to incense and candles, I place a chocolate at the shrine on special days. I replace the chocolate on the next special day with a new one while I consume the "old" one as part of the ceremony. The same is true for sharing black water, cognac, and other things. In the fall I place colored leaves at the shrine, in spring and summer fresh flowers, and during the winter I maintain the always blooming purple orchid (a year round practice). I also set extra places at the table on special days and share special food and drink.

Perhaps you already share quintessence with your disembodied loved one but refer to your ceremony by a different name. If you do not currently share quintessence, you might consider some form of sharing both to honor your disembodied loved one and to honor your embodied soul. Your embodied soul may whisper inspirations about sharing and if you listen carefully so may your disembodied loved one and other spirit realm helpers. Sharing quintessence is one of the keys to thinning the veil that many of us have established between the physical realm and spirit realm. Sharing quintessence sends your hopes, wishes, and intent to the spirit realm.

111 Things That Help Grieving: **#68**

Soulmates – Spiritmates

Many wisdom traditions describe the concept of soulmates. Two individuals connected at the level of their embodied souls. The connection transcends the embodied life time of soulmates as the connection is maintained in the spirit realm. Soulmate's connection flows across embodied lifetimes and is always, forever, and beyond. Some wisdom traditions describe soul families where the soul connections are shared by a larger group that might be called ancestors. Most wisdom traditions also describe one member of the soul family as primary or soulmate.

I have been blessed beyond measure in finding my soulmate during this lifetime. Where some relationships establish connections at a few energy levels, soulmates are connected at all levels even if the connections are not consciously experienced. The experience of finding your soulmate is one of coming home – knowing them in some subtle way across this and all other lifetimes. Always knowing the other and knowing that the other is the other half of oneself. When two embodied souls merge they experience the higher selves of both themselves and each other. The energy transcends the physical realm as does the experience. When we first met my embodied soul recognized and remembered my soulmate instantly. It took longer for my consciousness to process the metaphysical reality of my experience.

With the disembodiment of my soulmate, her soul returned to our spirit realm home to be reunited with other aspects of her higher self as well as the higher self of her soulmate and soul family. With her disembodiment, I converted the term "soulmate" to "spiritmate" to honor the transformation. I am aware that this may be interpreted as semantic word play; however, my intent is to acknowledge the transformation of my connection to my soulmate. I use both terms often as interchangeable but experience the subtle differences between them.

The disembodiment of my soulmate is the most traumatic experience of my embodied lifetime. I experienced the golden rainbow cocoon of our energy connections as damaged and beyond repair. At first I thought her half of our golden rainbow cocoon was a blackened shell or husk of its former glory. Over time I realized the damaged section of our golden rainbow cocoon was my half particularly at the levels of lower energy connections (see chakra cords/chakra connections, #11, page 31). My soulmate has transformed, transcended leaving behind very subtle energy connections that I was only vaguely able to "see" through the tears of my grief. For a long time, distorted by my tears, I believed Carol Susan's half of our golden rainbow cocoon was damaged. At four and one half years post-disembodiment, I can "see" somewhat better and experience the subtle reality of the "new" golden rainbow cocoon.

The disembodiment of my soulmate created a severing which I experienced as being cut in half. When she disembodied as the portal to the spirit realm opened and she was escorted to our spirit realm home by a large group of energy beings; her soul or spirit family – who could be described as angels; a portion of my embodied soul disembodied transforming to spirit just as she did so I could accompany her to our spirit realm home. My soulmate, now spiritmate, and the other energy beings welcomed me with compassionate love as they know that I needed to accompany my beloved soulmate home. Enough of my embodied soul remained in the physical realm to ensure that I can complete whatever life tasks, lesions, or purposes I have yet to do.

Before her disembodiment, I had not spent as much time or energy thinking about the energy connections between my soulmate and me as I was content to experience and enjoy our connections. After my heart was broken open with loss, laying bare my heart of hearts, improving my experience of the connections to the spirit realm has become one of my primary missions. Many of the things that help grieving are focused on ways to improve experiencing the subtle connections to the spirit realm.

Should your loss be that of your soulmate, may you find some measure of comfort, solace, and perhaps improved understanding of the intensity of the experience when viewed from the perspective of transformation. May the concept of the transformation of "soulmate" to "spiritmate" provides an increased understanding of the transcendence of your connection to the spirit realm.

Writing in 1930, Dion Fortune describes the transformation from soulmates to spiritmates even if she uses different language:

"It may seem like a strange thing to say, but true love is not emotional in its nature, but is an attitude of the soul towards life. True love is a spiritual radiation, like sunlight... To those who are united in spirit, death is but a temporary severance. There must be loneliness, and there must be burdens to be shouldered alone that were once shared by the other, but there is not that sense of spiritual annihilation which devastates those who have laid up their treasure where moth and rust corrupt. It is this inner certainty of an enduring bond which is the sheet-anchor in times of bereavement....When there is a real tuning of two souls, they are literally together on the Inner Planes, where to be of one mind is to be of one place....if there is a true spiritual union we remain in touch, wherever our bodies may be....the bond of spiritual union survives all severance whether of space or time and continues to inspire and to protect both of those who are held in its tie, upon whatever plane they may be...This spiritual communion continues uninterruptedly through the death of the body and all the after death experiences of the soul...When spiritual love is coming to us from the Inner Planes we have only to still the outer senses for a moment to hear it purling like the brook, a steady flow, coming to us all the time from the eternal and steadfast soul that has gone ahead to the Next Country. And we on our side, if we still love, may send out an equally steady flow to comfort our beloved."*

Dion Fortune

Dion Fortune, **Through the Gates of Death** (1930), republished as **Dion Fortune's Book of the Dead** by Weiser Books, 2005, pages 24-26.

111 Things That Help Grieving: **#69**

Soulmates – Guardian Angels

The concept of shared past lives provides an explanation for the strong attraction and sense of having already or always known the person of your soulmate. Spending many life times together strengthens the energy connection between two soulmates. However, the concept of shared past lives does not provide an explanation for knowing my soulmate when she was a small child or that somehow she knew me when I was a small child. Based upon golden dreams and other inspirations, I suggest that the relationship of soulmates is even more complex that sharing past lives. Soulmates are one another's guardian angel – at least one of a number of guardian angels. An aspect of one's higher self functions as one of the guardian angels watching over one's soulmate, whispering inspirations, and providing the energy of protection, acceptance, and love. The relationship of your soulmate as one of your guardian angels does not end with the disembodiment of your soulmate.

Perhaps the aspect of one's higher self functioning as one of the guardian angels (energy beings) of your soulmate is not directly accessible to your conscious mind; however, your embodied soul accesses the relationship with ease. That the awareness of the relationship is only vaguely and infrequently remembered, if at all, may be related both to one's belief system, as well as a cultural bias that discourages the expression and experience of most forms of metaphysical experience.

With an expanded opening to your heart of hearts as a result of the disembodiment of your soulmate, you may have a similar experience to mine in remembering past lives with your soulmate (perhaps in gazing at a photograph or in golden dreams). You may at other moments of inspiration become aware of an aspect of your soulmate as your guardian angel and realize at the same time an aspect of your higher self is one of the guardian angels of your soulmate. This awareness has provided me with comfort during the black nights of my soul after the disembodiment of my soulmate.

Should these concepts not resonate with you, as the **I Ching** advises, there is no harm and therefore no blame.

111 Things That Help Grieving: **#70**

Soror Mystica : Alchemy

In alchemical literature the soror mystica is often defined as mystic sister. In psychological literature, specifically Jungian, soror mystica is described as the soul, anima, moon, silver, and other aspects of the feminine.

"Of these parts two are the artificers, who in the symbolical realm are Sol and Luna, in the human the adept and his soror mystica, and in the psychological realm the masculine consciousness and the feminine unconscious (anima)."*

C.G. Jung

One of the clearest depictions of the relationship of the male alchemist and his female counterpart is found in the book **Mutus Liber**, translated Mute Book. The **Mutus Liber**, first published in 1677, contains fifteen wood block prints with no text. The fifteen pictures reveal the soror mystica as an equal partner to the male alchemist. The female alchemist also appears to provide inspiration for the pair as she interacts with the spirit realm energies of transformation.

"One interpretation of this would be that these two figures, the male and female partners, are in fact parts of the individual soul of the alchemist undertaking this work. However, equally valid is the viewpoint that the Great Work cannot be achieved except by such a partnership of the alchemist and his Soror Mystica. The idea of the Mystical Marriage and the Chemical Wedding is an important element in the esoteric alchemical tradition."**

Adam McLean

The soror mystica is all of those aspects described above and more. The soror mystica is the soulmate of the alchemist and an alchemist in her own right. The female alchemist is an equal partner as well as the source of inspiration for the pair. In alchemical symbols the pair are depicted as king and queen who at different phases in the alchemical processes are contained in a giant crucible which is being heated to a high temperature burning off the impure aspects of the royal couple refining them to enable their transformation to the next level in the alchemical process.

I often described our golden rainbow cocoon to Carol Susan, which at times transformed into a golden crucible heated by our subtle fires until it seemed black and at other times silver-white. She always enjoyed the image of our being roasted in the crucible, refining, and improving both ourselves and each other. That is not to say that sometimes the subtle fires were not hot as hell and painful to experience. After each episode of our alchemical process the crucible would transform into our golden cocoon.

To provide an improved "knowing" or personal experience of alchemy looking at alchemical drawings and pictures will provide a wealth of information that will resonate at some level of your being – most likely as nourishment for your embodied soul. The alchemical images are food for your embodied soul assisting the embodied soul to transmit information to the often skeptical and resistant ego system. If you have not explored alchemical images, I encourage you to do so. An excellent place to start would be Adam McLean's web site (alchemywebsite.com) or levity.com/alchemy.

That your soulmate has disembodied not only does not terminate the alchemical process but takes the alchemical process to a much more complex level across realms and beyond the constraints of the physical realm. Should the alchemical images not resonate with you, as the **I Ching** advises, no harm no blame. One does need to suspend rational (read critical) judgment to be inspired by alchemical images.

May you find the concept of the soror mystica as another term for soulmate, as well as the images of alchemy and the alchemical processes of male and female alchemists as equal partners to be of value in understanding the dark night of the soul as part of the alchemical process of transformation. The primary image is the pair of alchemists as equal partners and soulmates. It is not necessary to learn all of the alchemical terms and processes to be impacted by the symbolism of alchemy at the level of your embodied soul. Along with honoring the dead, it is also important to provide nourishment to our embodied soul as a way of honoring our soul, both the aspect we are embodied with, as well as other larger aspects.

Marie-Louise von Franz. **Alchemy: An Introduction to the Symbolism and the Psychology**, Inner City Books, 1980.

*C.G. Jung. **Mysteruim Coniunctionis**, Collected Works, Volume 14, Princeton University Press, 1963, pages 153-154.

Adam McLean. **A Commentary on the Mutus Liber, Phanes Press, 1991, page 57.

111 Things That Help Grieving: **#71**

Talking With My Spirit Companion

I continue to talk with my companion now in her spirit form. I write to her every day in journal entries. I tell her things both out loud and mind to mind. Now and then I become still enough to listen and hear her subtle spirit voice in reply. Most of the time my ability to hear her subtle spirit voice seems impaired, as I am still too dark, heavy, and raw to achieve the stillness necessary to hear her subtle whispers. Even though I do not often remember my golden dreams, she speaks to me mind to mind in the golden dreams I remember. During some of the most intense periods of grieving my beloved's voice has spoken mind to mind giving me a message to assist me in my struggles coping with the loss of her embodied form.

I find great comfort and healing from talking with my spirit companion. I find even greater comfort and healing when I hear her subtle whispers, clear spoken messages, and golden dreams. While her mind to mind messages are always wonderful healing experiences, being in the presence of her loving energy is a blessing beyond words.

Likely you are already talking with your disembodied loved one. Should you not be talking with your disembodied loved one, consider having a conversation in whatever way seems comfortable to you. Perhaps your subtle listening skills are, like mine, somewhat underdeveloped, so you have difficulties clearly hearing your loved one's responses. May you continue to develop your listening skills so you can better receive inspirations, messages, and best of all, the healing energy of spirit realm love.

111 Things That Help Grieving: **#72**

Support of Family and Friends

The support of family, friends, and colleagues after the disembodiment of a loved one offers a measure of solace during the dark hours, days, weeks, months, and years to follow. As there are few experts at coping with personal loss, some family, friends, and colleagues will be able to be supportive close up while others will not be comfortable witnessing your grief and mourning or sharing their own. Some will, in fact, be so uncomfortable as to disappear. While it is difficult to not take their coping strategy of disappearance personally; they are most likely doing the very best that they can within their limitations. Witnessing your grief and sharing their own is just too much so they take distance. In a culture that works hard to deny aging, dying, and death; few are "good" at being with dying, death, and the bereaved left behind after the disembodiment of a beloved one. Family, friends, and colleagues who understand the need to honor the dead are also able to honor the living in their grief.

It needs to be mentioned that as there are few experts in living and dying, some folk are more "unripe" or primitive in their development than others. Some will offer encouragement, subtle to harsh, to "just get on with your life" more or less acting as if nothing has happened which is, of course, a reflection of their way of coping. They have fully embraced the denial of death and anything that reminds them of the delusional nature of their death denying reality is threatening. I strongly recommend that you stay as far away from these "unripe" people as you can. I also hope that they are not your closest family members and/or closest friends. The concept of honoring the dead may be alien to these people with the result being since they do not honor the dead they dishonor both the dead and the living.

May you be blessed with family, friends, and colleagues who are able to be with you offering their support, love, and sharing in your grief as well as sharing their own grief. Immediate family and close friends will need your support, love, and sharing as much as you need theirs.

111 Things That Help Grieving: **#73**

Residual Energy

Things that your disembodied loved one used, wore, treasured, and/or gave to you as well as things you shared retain the smallest amount of your loved ones energy. While you may or may not be aware of the energy at a conscious level, your subtle senses (I call "metasenses") register the energy. The concept of residual energy of "things" may provide you with valuable understanding and awareness. If you are open to the energy you may find the "things" provide a small measure of comfort. For me, many items are charged with my beloved's energy. I can experience the energy and treasure the energy associated with the object. The objects themselves are not the treasure – the treasure is the smallest particles of her energy remaining. The energy associated with the "thing" assists in activating and amplifying memories associated with the object intensifying the experience.

Therefore if you, like me, have little to no interest in disposing of your disembodied love ones things do not be self-critical or harsh in your judgment of yourself. You are likely finding a measure of comfort in the residual energy remaining even if you do not fully understand why. I am in no rush to "purge" the personal items of my beloved. I am using any number of her things both as a way to honor the dead and experience her subtle energy. Of course the smallest particles of her energy only provide a small measure of comfort but that is the reality of my experience and will have to be enough.

If the "things" left behind by your disembodied love one "creep you out" by all means remove them from your presence. As the **I Ching** advises there is no harm and no blame. Without understanding the concept of residual energy the energy of the "things" may be interpreted as "spooky."

Perhaps the concept of residual energy will provide you with a small measure of comfort as your attachment to certain "things" is both a way of honoring the dead and honoring your embodied lives together.

111 Things That Help Grieving: **#74**

Grief Journey/Healing Journey

For the first few years when I read about grief being a journey of healing the concept irritated the hell out of me. I was much too raw, dark, and heavy to consider grief a journey, much less a journey of healing. When I read about grief as a journey I would speculate about how far removed the writer was from the moment of disembodiment of their loved one. I also wondered how many and how strong were their connections. Somewhere around two and a half years after the disembodiment of my beloved soulmate I started to realize that many of my activities were attempts to regain my balance and restore some kind of equilibrium after this traumatic loss. I decided that perhaps reestablishing some kind of equilibrium describes a form of healing. I still did not like the idea of a healing journey or grief journey. If the idea of a grief journey or healing journey seems ridiculous or even ludicrous to you, you may prefer to skip this thing that helps grieving for now. As the **I Ching** advises there is no harm - no blame.

My image of riding the dragon named grief, then being swallowed by the dragon named grief, and swallowing the dragon named grief suggests a journey into the dark night of the soul, a night sea journey during a raging thunderstorm, and experiencing the hellfires of grief. This does not describe the usual mythic image of the warrior-hero who sets out to slay the dragon and rescue the damsel in distress. In this journey, the bereaved is a wounded person with a broken heart, holding on by a thread, with the wounds hemorrhaging energy. The grief journey is an encounter with death and loss with the bereaved being the one in distress. The grief journey is not the standard mythic hero's journey. The image is a journey toward regaining some type of balance or equilibrium, which seems a monstrous task.

Eventually I realized that my grieving and active grief work are attempts to cope with the trauma of loss that might be considered a dark journey into the belly of the dragon named grief. The 111 things that help grieving are each an aspect of my grief work, with the early objective being to regain my equilibrium. With good fortune beyond measure, the bereaved person experiences golden dreams, subtle messages, and inspirations. Remembering these experiences provides powerful healing and takes the grief journey to a new level. The experiencing of the disembodied loved one in golden dreams and other subtle messages begins a transformation as I realize the disembodied loved one is still present only in a more subtle form. As the bereaved becomes more attuned to the spirit realm, the transformation continues. The black dragon named grief starts to also reveal glimpses of the golden rainbow energy of love. Looking with eyes of loss the dragon named grief continues to look black and traumatizing. Looking with eyes of love, the dragon can be seen as the bridge to the spirit realm and eternal love. In my grief work, the golden rainbow energy experiences are much fewer than the black experiences of loss; however, they do suggest a different reality of experience. The bereaved then becomes, not the out dated warrior-hero, but a spirit realm seeker who begins to befriend the dragon who offers wisdom and access to the spirit realm. Embracing the dragon named grief is an intensely painful, yet healing experience. It also leads towards the discovery of one's soul's needs and purposes. Embracing the dragon named grief is not easy work, often seeming to produce more pain than healing. I cannot suggest what the next level of the journey might be. My intuition suggests, as a result of glimpses of the spirit realm, an experience beyond transformation to transmutation. This is purely conjecture as my experiences with the spirit realm are far less frequent that hoped for.

111 Things That Help Grieving: **#75**

Spirit Warrior

"Warriorship here does not refer to making war on others. Aggression is the source of our problems, not the solution. Here the word *warrior* is taken from the Tibetan "parvo" and literally means "one who is brave." Warriorship in this context is the tradition of human bravery, or the tradition of fearlessness."*

Chogyam Trungpa

Many wisdom traditions use the term "spiritual warrior," while others use the terms "spiritual pilgrim" or "spiritual seeker." Whichever the term, there are shared attributes which include courageousness, fearlessness, open-hearted, loving kindness, perseverance, seeking one's higher nature, seeking one's calling or soul's purpose, and the willingness to share and help others.

In experiencing loss, grief, and grieving, the spirit warrior does not use the automatic responses of fight, flight, or freezing, but rather embraces the awful reality of loss and the experiences of grief and grieving. Embracing the reality of loss requires courage to encounter the hellfires of grief, the intense emotional flooding, and knowing the fragile nature of our embodied life as a result of experiencing the moment of the disembodiment of a loved one.

I prefer to use the term "spirit seeker" rather than "spirit warrior" or "spirit pilgrim," but the difference is one of semantics as the concepts are more or less interchangeable. Perhaps I prefer the term "spirit seeker" as I often find myself reproaching myself for not being much of a spirit warrior. I certainly have the soft heart attribute, as well as perseverance and seeking a path with heart or my soul's purpose(s) or calling(s). My limitations center on fearlessness, courageousness, and equanimity, which often seem to be lacking.

The experience of the loss of my beloved soulmate has created a dark night of the soul in which I have been conducting a life review under the worst possible conditions as experienced through my broken heart. My priorities have been radically readjusted. My experience of the reality of death has become intensely intimate. Even when I experience a moment of two of disbelief, the awful reality quickly returns.

I am not suggesting that embracing the awful reality of loss is an easy or quick process, quite the contrary, as I believe it to be the most painful and life altering of human experiences. The embracing of loss and the resulting experiences of grief and grieving require the courage of a spirit warrior, following a path with heart, and the increase urgency to fulfill one's soul's purpose. The spirit warrior approaches life with an attitude of loving kindness towards oneself and others, sharing and helping others, and cultivating the higher aspects of one's true nature. Being or becoming a spirit warrior requires moving beyond the automatic responses of fighting, fleeing, or freezing to encounter loss, grief, and grieving and to persevere until the journey through grief has become first matched by loved and then transformed by love.

May the concept of spirit warrior, spirit seeker, or spirit pilgrim provides you with a way of seeing your dark night of the soul and grieving process from a different and more positive perspective. The perspective I have termed *eyes of love* rather than *eyes of loss*. Adopting the values and attributes of a spirit warrior will not reduce the hellfires of grief resulting from the loss of your loved one. In fact, adopting the values, attributes, and attitude of a spirit warrior will most likely intensify the experience of grief and grieving as you fully embrace the awful reality of your experience. While it sounds like an obvious truism, the thing that helps grieving is grieving.

Even when you falter as a spirit warrior and feel yourself not measuring up to the ideal, you will persevere and that your courage, open heartedness, loving kindness, and seeking will prove to be good enough for you to realize your soul's purpose and discover your higher self in the spirit realm along with your disembodied loved ones.

*Chogyam Trungpa, **Shambhala: The Sacred Path of the Warrior**, Shambhala Publications, 1984, page 7.

111 Things That Help Grieving: **#76**

Basic Bodily Functions

The stress of grief can and often does create dysfunctions of basic bodily functions. Difficulty sleeping, loss of appetite, not drinking enough water and becoming dehydrated, and/or difficulties with elimination may all be experienced during grief. The opposite extreme may also be experienced as in over eating, over indulging in comfort food, excessive use of alcohol or other chemicals, and excessive sleeping. While the time after the loss of a loved one is a very difficult time to monitor and correct serious disruptions in basic bodily functions, the process of grieving will less likely result in physical problems if attention is given to maintaining adequate sleep, hydration, adequate nutrition, and regular elimination. Should the basic bodily functions become seriously disrupted, seeking medical intervention is recommended.

It is more difficult to cope with grief if sleep deprived, dehydrated, malnourished, and/or constipated. While the time after the loss of a loved one is the worst time to be concerned about self care, focus on maintaining basic bodily functions is necessary to prevent grief from becoming complicated with medical issues. The other things that help grieving are maximized in effectiveness if the basic needs of the physical body are reasonably met. Most of the things that help grieving focus on emotions, mind, soul, and spirit; however, if the vessel or body is neglected and/or abused coping with loss becomes complicated with physical stresses increasing the risk of adding physical illness to the experience of grief.

I recommend the book **One Spirit Medicine** by Alberto Villoldo as it addresses the needs of the body, mind, and spirit. Regular medical evaluations to assist in monitoring your physical condition are recommended. Should you experience problems maintaining basic bodily functions, an urgent evaluation by your doctor is recommended. Maintaining physical health provides the basic foundation for using the other things that help grieving.

May you maintain your basic bodily functions within normal limits and avoid physical complications. Should self care not prove to be adequate, the resources of medical professionals as well as other professional helpers/healers becomes essential.

For additional information about **One Spirit Medicine** by Alberto Villoldo see thing that helps grieving #99, page 250.

111 Things That Help Grieving: **#77**

Energy Work/Energy Healing

Energy work or energy healing can provide healing benefits at anytime; however, the benefits are increased substantially with the experience of grieving. The severing of energy ties to the physically embodied loved one is traumatic on many levels – physical, emotional, psychological, mental, and spiritual. Loss produces significant energy issues including lack of grounding, energy loss through damaged energy connections, and difficulties accessing higher levels of energy. Most likely being poorly grounded, difficulty accessing higher spirit realms, and energy loss from severed connections occur simultaneously. Energy flows become blocked, scrambled, reversed, stagnant, and hemorrhaging.

While energy work or energy healing cannot fully remove the impact of loss, energy work can assist in grounding and provide energy first aid to severed and leaking energy systems, as well as improve connections to higher energy levels. There are numerous energy treatment systems including those of Donna Eden, Barbara Ann Brennan, and Alberto Villoldo. I was fortunate to find an energy healer trained and experienced in the energy illumination work of Alberto Villoldo. Improved grounding was one of the first energy healing interventions, as I had become disconnected, focusing more on accessing the spirit realm and ignoring most everything else. Addressing the damaged energy systems was also a top priority both by energy infusions (energy illuminations) and by restoring damaged energy systems as much as possible. Ignoring energy systems during the trauma of loss protracts achieving balance and increases the likelihood that energy issues become converted into physical issues, further complicating bereavement.

Consider the services of an energy healer. While there are many energy healing traditions, those that I have studied and experienced include those of Alberto Villoldo, Donna Eden, and Barbara Ann Brennan.

Brief summaries of several books by Alberto Villoldo are listed as things that help grieving: **Shaman, Healer, Sage** (#97, page 247); **A Shaman's Miraculous Tools for Healing** (#98, page 249); and **One Spirit Medicine** (#99, page 250). For a brief introduction to the work of Barbara Ann Brennan see Chakras and other subtle energy systems (#10, page 29) and Chakra Cords/Chakra Connections (#11, page 31).

111 Things That Help Grieving: **#78**

Grief Counseling

After the disembodiment of my beloved both the family doctor and nurse practitioner recommended grief counseling. A hospice grief counselor called to check in and offer their services. She suggested I was likely feeling very raw. I agreed and was supported by her call and the use of the term "raw' as raw accurately described one aspect of the reality of my experience. I adopted the term "raw" and added "dark" and "heavy" to more fully describe how I was feeling. There was also massive denial, disbelief, intense despair, intense longing, intense missing, and a host of other emotions.

I decided to schedule a visit with the hospice grief counselor. She was supportive, empathetic, and compassionate. She listened, offered support, and suggested resources some of which are listed as books that have helped grieving. We talked about my ceremonies and my struggle to cope with the major trauma of my loss. I went to grief counseling for around four months and discontinued when I left the area to spend some time with my daughter in another state.

I recommend grief counseling even if you have a large support system and believe you are doing alright with your grieving. Grief counselors are trained to assist people who have experienced the major trauma of loss of a loved one. I experienced grief counseling and the grief counselor as one of the things that help grieving. At a time of the most significant negative experience of my life, I was blessed with the support of family and friends as well as professional helpers and healers. In addition to the family doctor, nurse practitioner, and grief counselor; I also received assistance from a massage therapist, acupuncturist, and energy healer. Give yourself permission to seek professional helpers and healers to assist you with the most stressful and traumatic experience of your life.

111 Things That Help Grieving: **#79**

Massage Therapy

Massage therapy from a massage therapist with strong healing gifts is another form of energy work and energy healing. Massage works on the physical body but also impacts more subtle energy systems. I was fortunate to find a massage therapist who was a gifted and intuitive healer in addition to being a highly skilled massage therapist. I can state from experience that not all massage therapists provide the same level of healing work.

The trauma and stresses of loss are often held in the physical body resulting in tight muscles and organ systems as well as poor energy flows. Therapeutic massage loosens bound muscular systems, frees energy, and assists subtle energy systems in their healing repairs. I highly recommend considering therapeutic massage from a massage therapists with "healing hands." Consider finding a massage therapist who is also an energy healer. Massage therapy is an excellent compliment to other forms of energy work and energy healing.

111 Things That Help Grieving: **#80**

Acupuncture

Acupuncture is an ancient healing tradition which provides interventions (needles) at appropriate locations on a large and complex grid of subtle energy channels (meridians). Acupuncture is an energy healing tradition that stimulates energy points on the physical body as well as subtle energy bodies to improve the flow of energy. The meridians are subtle energy channels that can be blocked or damaged and corrected by proper stimulation (acupuncture). Acupuncture is a subtle healing tradition which can complement and enhance other healing traditions. I highly recommend the combination of energy healing, therapeutic massage, and acupuncture as they enhance and maximize the healing benefits of one another.

111 Things That Help Grieving: **#81**

Grief and Disease

Grief is the natural human response to loss and is expressed in a wide variety of ways. Grief is not a disease or an illness in spite of the tendency to view grief as a problem in need of medical intervention. Converting the natural response of bereavement following the loss of a loved one into a pathological condition suggests something is wrong with the person because they are grieving. Grief does not fit the disease model. The tendency to force fit grief into the medical model denies the reality of one's experience and demeans the loss which created the grief. The only way to avoid grief resulting from the loss of your loved one is to not outlive your loved one.

One does not cure grief or get over the reality of the experience of loss. With time and grief work, the intensity of bereavement may diminish; however, there is no cure for the loss while embodied. Grief resulting from the loss of a loved one is one of the most stressful of life's experiences, if not **the** most stressful. Stress, if not managed, can result in the development of stress related symptoms which may eventually manifest as disease. In order to manage the stress of loss and the resulting grief, it is necessary to grieve. Grieving honors the dead and the living. Doing the necessary grief work after the trauma of loss moves the bereaved person towards achieving equilibrium.

Attempting to avoid grief forces grief and all of the energy associated with grief underground often with undesirable consequences. Suppressing grief creates an environment more conducive to converting grief, the natural human response to loss, into a pathological condition. Directly experiencing the reality of one's situation and expressing grief improves the slow process of moving towards equilibrium. With some measure of equilibrium, the conditions for transformation began to be realized. Considering grief an illness or disease does not create a healthy environment for achieving equilibrium or for creating the conditions necessary for transformation.

Considering grief to be an illness or disease means grief needs to be treated, fixed, and cured. The culture has little tolerance for grieving and offers a multitude of "fixes" to cure the griever of their condition. What helps grievers is support, honoring their grief, honoring their loss, and honoring their dead. Since the loss of loved ones is a nature human experience there is no value converting the experience into a disease or illness any more than it is to consider death a disease or illness. The only "cure" for the loss of a loved one is grief and grieving.

May you experience grief and grieving as a natural human response to the loss of your loved one. While it is difficult to achieve separation and independence from the culture's aversion to dying, death, and grief; may you be able to honor your disembodied loved one, achieve equilibrium, and experience the transformational experience of golden dreams and other messages from your disembodied loved one. I hope you have family, friends, colleagues, and helpers that support you, honor your grief, and honor your dead.

111 Things That Help Grieving: **#82**

Gratitude

Early in my bereavement I was more focused on my loss than gratitude. I was grateful my soulmate and I rediscovered one another and spent thirty-four years embodied together; however, my focus was from eyes of loss. My experience of loss left me dark, raw, and heavy with grief and grieving. I know that we had been blessed with an intense and powerful connection as embodied souls. I realized when embodied connections were severed, the resulting experience of loss would be of equal intensity. Early after my beloved's disembodiment, I treasured the embodied connections almost to the exclusion of all else spending large amounts of time and energy looking back, remembering, and reminiscing. I slowly became aware that many of the memories were of loving moments. While my ongoing life review included more than an adequate amount of dark moments, it was the golden moments filled with love that sustained me during the darkest times.

In addition to being grateful beyond words for the years shared embodied together, I am even more grateful for moments shared now that my beloved has changed forms. I have been blessed beyond measure to experience her spirit presence. One of my early images is of a large golden rainbow being, who I immediately recognized as my beloved in her spirit form, holding my broken hearts together with her loving touch. I am grateful beyond words for golden dreams shared with my beloved. Golden dreams have provided intensely powerful healing energy. I am grateful to remember some of my visits to the spirit realm and grateful for the assistance of all my helpers.

I have written the thing that helps grieving "gratitude" last of the one hundred and eleven things that help grieving as a way of expressing my gratitude for all of the support provided by family and friends, both embodied and disembodied, especially my beloved Carol Susan and all of our helpers. Experiencing gratitude and expressing gratitude is a powerful healing force. Words spoken and unspoken have power and the expression of gratitude in whatever form communicates appreciation for being blessed beyond measure with love.

May you experience and express gratitude to your loved ones in whatever form you are comfortable. Licking my woundedness with words is one of the ways I have worked to heal my broken heart after the disembodiment of my soulmate. I am grateful for inspirations and subtle messages that have assisted me in the discovery of things that help grieving and in distilling them into a concentrated form.

May you be able to remember and realize all of the things for which you are grateful and that your gratitude finds a suitable form of expression. Gratitude does not remove the reality of loss or erase the experience of a broken heart. The awareness and expression of gratitude provides the healing force of love. May you be blessed with the awareness of the spirit presence of your disembodied loved one and that you are also blessed beyond measure with golden dreams, subtle spirit realm messages, and inspirations. Gratitude flows naturally from a broken and therefore open heart that is filled with love. May you be able to realize and express the gratitude that flows from the love within your heart of hearts.

111 Things That Help Grieving

"We read books to find out who we are. What other people...do and think and feel...is an essential guide to our understanding of what we ourselves are and may become."

Ursula K. Le Guin

Section Four

Book Resources

Before the disembodiment of my beloved Carol Susan, I read a wide variety of books. After her disembodiment, my interests in reading became laser focused to exclusively grief, grieving, and bereavement books. I read extensively but only self help grief books, grief resource books, grief memoirs, and grief poems. I had no interest in reading anything else. My research suggests this focused reading of grief books is a common experience.

Over time, I added books on healing, energy healing, and alchemy. I discovered when rereading books read years earlier that I read them with new eyes, as well as with an intensity that was not present before. Sharing in the grief experiences provided by the words of others provides comfort, solace, and a crude way to validate one's experience of loss, grief, and grieving. While each person's grief experiences are uniquely individual, there are common features, themes, and landscapes so the grief experiences of one can provide assistance to others.

The eighteen books included in Section Four have provided me the most assistance, benefit, and healing of the many bereavement and related books I have read over the last four and one half years.

111 Things That Help Grieving: **#83**

Book Resource 1:

Carol Staudacher. **A Time To Grieve: Meditations for Healing After the Death of a Loved One.** HarperCollins Publishers, 1994, 248 pages, $14.99 paper bound.

A Time To Grieve is the first book recommended by my grief counselor. I have given **A Time To Grieve** to family and friends. Each has expressed their appreciation. I continue to keep **A Time To Grieve** nearby and have reread it multiple times. My copy is underlined, highlighted, tabbed, and dog eared.

"Some survivors try to think their way through grief. That doesn't work. Grief is a relearning process, a discovery process, a healing process. We cannot release or discover or heal by the use of our minds alone. The brain must follow the heart at a respectful distance. It is our hearts that ache when a loved one dies. It is our emotions that are most drastically affected. Certainly the mind suffers, the mind recalls, the mind may plot and plan and wish, but it is the heart that will blaze the trail through the thicket of grief." (page 7)

A Time To Grieve starts each page with a quote from a survivor, followed by a quote by a published author, then a meditation on the two quotes, and ending with a positive affirmation statement. **A Time To Grieve** is organized into three phases:

retreating, working through, and resolving. Most of the topics are presented in one page with some being a bit longer. The book can be opened and read at any page or topic.

If you have not read **A Time To Grieve**, I highly recommend you do so no matter where you might be in your grief and bereavement process. I also recommend giving copies to family members and friends even if they are not readers.

"The most I ever did for you, was to outlive you
But that is much."
      Edna St. Vincent Millay (page 47)

"Take my word for it, the saddest thing
under the sky is a soul incapable of sadness."
      Countess De Gasparin (page 62)

111 Things That Help Grieving: **#84**

Book Resource 2

Doreen Virtue and James Van Praagh. *How To Heal A Grieving Heart.* Hay House, Inc., 2013, 120 pages, $16.95 hard bound.

How To Heal A Grieving Heart is a beautiful small book with a brief healing message on each page as well as lovely photographs of butterflies and flowers. Written by a clairvoyant psychotherapist working with the angelic realm and a spirit medium, the material presented on each page is a meditation written to comfort mind, body, heart, and embodied soul. Doreen Virtue and James Van Praagh write in the introduction to *How To Heal A Grieving Heart* that they wrote the book they wished they had during their own grieving processes. I also wish I had *How To Heal A Grieving Heart* earlier in my grieving process. I often open *How To Heal A Grieving Heart* at random and read a few pages. *How To Heal A Grieving Heart* is an excellent resource that fully acknowledges the spirit realm and provides healing energies from both the physical and spirit realms.

For additional information about books published by Doreen Virtue and books published by James Van Praagh see their websites listed below.

Doreen Virtue (www.angeltherapy.com)
James Van Praagh (www.vanpraagh.com)

Doreen Virtue. *Healing with the Angels: How the Angels Can Assist You in Every Area of Your Life.* Hay House, 1999, 191 pages, $13.95 soft cover.

"When we have conversations with our deceased loved ones, we help them ease their souls and bring peace to ourselves in the process." (page 95)
"Our relationships with our loved ones don't end with their death. The relationship merely changes form. As a psychotherapist and clairvoyant medium, I help my clients maintain healthy relationships with their loved ones on the other side. Healthy post-death relationships are important for the sakes of souls on both sides of the veil of death." (page 97)

James Van Praagh. *Growing Up In Heaven: The Eternal Connection Between Parent and Child.* Harper Collins, 2011, 214 pages, $25.95 hard cover.

"Within our soul family are our soul mates. I believe that we each have many soul mates, not just one, and that these souls have shared special relationships in various incarnations. Soul mates usually feel and overwhelming sense of being 'simpatico,' if you will, that is instantly recognizable. Soul mates share a soul memory and have similar values, attractions, likes, and dislikes…. **Remember, too that soul mates continue to work with you on the spiritual levels once they depart from this lifetime.**" (pages 76-77)

111 Things That Help Grieving: **#85**

Book Resource 3

Ashley Davis Bush. **Transcending Loss: Understanding the Lifelong Impact of Grief and How to Make It Meaningful.** Berkley Books/Penguin, 1997, 280 pages, $16.00 paper bound.

"Our losses affect us irrevocably. When a loved one dies, the deepest loss of all, a part of us dies too and life will never, ever be the same again."
Introduction, page xiii

"Grieving is not a short-term process; it's not even a long term process; it's a *lifelong* process."
Introduction, page xv

Transcending Loss is a gentle, kind, and compassionate book describing the lifelong impact of grief. Ashley Davis Bush, LCSW; a licensed psychotherapist and grief counselor in private practice; describes grief as lifelong and suggests grief may create the need to transcend loss and find meaning. She interviewed fifty people an average of five years after their loss to determine their "long term adaptation to loss." Throughout the book, Ashley Bush uses the voices of the grievers she interviewed to illustrate her concepts. **Transcending Loss** starts with a description of the three stages of acute grief which Ashley Bush calls shock, disorganization, and reconstruction. Part I: The Initial Grief Journey is an excellent presentation of the acute stages of grief in fifty-nine pages. The remainder of the book is devoted to looking beyond the acute phases at the lifelong impact of grief. In Part II, Ashley Bush identifies two lifelong phases beyond the acute stages of grief. She calls the first **synthesis** defined as "integrating life with loss" and the second **transcendence** defined as "making meaning out of loss." Part III offers ways to make loss meaningful and Parts IV and V focus on difficulties reaching the stage of transcendence and potential solutions when stuck.

Transcending Loss should be read by everyone who has experienced the loss of a loved one as it is the single best book to present both the lifelong perspective of loss as well as excellent suggestions to assist in transcending loss. I have recommended **Transcending Loss** to a number of family and friends all of whom have found the book to be an excellent resource.

Additional information about **Transcending Loss** and other resources provided by Ashley Davis Bush are available at www.ashleydavisbush.com.

111 Things That Help Grieving: **#86**

Book Resource 4

Tom Golden. *The Way Men Heal*. G.H. Publishing, 2013, 58 pages, $7.99 paper bound.

Tom Golden, LCSW, started his career as a therapist in a death and dying counseling center. He found his traditional training in talk therapy was not effective with the majority of men. In 1996, he published **Swallowed by a Snake: The Gift of the Masculine Side of Healing**, presenting his discoveries along with a comprehensive presentation of grief and grieving. **Swallowed by a Snake** was revised in 2000 and will be described in book resource 5, (things that help grieving #87 page 222).

Golden describes the masculine side of healing as a different mode of healing from the feminine side of healing. *The Way Men Heal* is a condensed version (58 pages) with the primary focus on the masculine side of healing and how it is both largely invisible and often misunderstood. Golden notes in his experience 75% of men use the masculine side of healing as their primary mode of healing as do 20% of women. The feminine mode of healing focuses on talking and emotional release shared with others. The masculine mode of healing is action focused with the expression of emotions and talking about pain and suffering taboo. Golden describes three additional reasons why the masculine side of healing is largely invisible as involving traditional male roles of providing and protecting, male dominance hierarchy, and brain and hormonal differences, specifically testosterone.

Golden identifies three action modes of the masculine side of healing: practical action, creative action, and thinking action. Actions include dedication of one's work, pilgrimages, scholarships, charities, memorials, music, art, writing, journaling, and reading. Golden provides three primary examples of each of the three action modes. The book also includes sections of tips for women and therapists.

The Way Men Heal is a small but powerful book describing the differences in masculine and feminine ways of dealing with loss, grief, and healing. Written to provide a better understanding of people who prefer action to talking and emoting, ***The Way Men Heal*** is an excellent resource. For those whose primary mode of healing is feminine, ***The Way Men Heal*** provides excellent insights, improved awareness, and better understanding resulting in improved compassion for those who are primarily action focused and do not easily deal with loss by sharing words or emotions. For those whose primary mode of healing is masculine, action focused, ***The Way Men Heal*** provides validation that actions are a legitimate mode of healing.

For additional information about Tom Golden, LCSW and his work see www.webhealing.com

111 Things That Help Grieving: **#87**

Book Resource 5

Thomas R. Golden. *Swallowed by a Snake: The Gift of the Masculine Side of Healing.* Second Edition. G.H. Publishing, 1996/2000, 173 pages, $13.93 paper bound.

Thomas Golden, LCSW, is a psychotherapist specializing in healing from loss. *Swallowed by a Snake* was first published in 1996 and expanded in the second edition published in 2000 after the disembodiment of his father. Golden uses the image of being swallowed by a snake to describe the experience of loss and grief.

In the first section, Golden focuses on the experience of being swallowed describing grief, how to evaluate grief, and an excellent chapter on the value of establishing rituals to assist coping with the chaos created by loss. Regarding ritual Golden indicates: "In our culture, where there are almost no sanctioned rituals for healing grief, we are forced into a position of having to create our own rituals, many times without the help of others." (page 33)

The focus of section two is getting out of the snake. Golden describes the emotional aspects of grief, gender differences, and the masculine gift of healing through action. Focusing on the active male mode of healing, Golden discusses the need to become aware of grief to enable "standing in your tension." Golden recommends a variety of rituals to cope with loss and grief. The chapters on gender differences and the masculine gift of healing through action provide excellent information based on Golden's experience as a psychotherapist focusing on loss and grief. Golden estimates that 75% of men and 20% of women use the active mode of healing as their primary mode of healing rather than the feminine mode of relating (talking and emoting). Golden indicates the action mode is largely invisible and poorly understood leading others to assume the person is not grieving. Golden summarizes gender differences in his book **The Way Men Heal** (book resource 4, #86, page 220).

Section three presents cultural differences in grief and grieving which Golden terms "the ground of the battle." Golden states: "Our own culture provides fertile soil for a variety of things, but not for grief. The 'grief soil' of our culture could be likened to a desert. The denial of death and grief is massive, and this makes grieving difficult." (page 97)

Section four is an Epilogue added after the death of his father providing his personal experiences expressing, standing in his tension, and healing his grief.

Swallowed by a Snake is an excellent resource providing a comprehensive overview of the experience of loss and grief with emphasis on the masculine mode of healing through action rather than the feminine mode of relating (talking and emoting). **The Way Men Heal** provides an excellent summary and can be read as a standalone resource. **Swallowed by a Snake** is a more comprehensive resource than **The Way Men Heal**. I recommend reading both **The Way Men Heal** and **Swallowed by a Snake.**

For additional information on Tom Golden, LCSW, and his work see www.webhealing.com

111 Things That Help Grieving: #88

Book Resource 6

Joan Halifax. ***Being With Dying: Cultivating Compassion and Fearlessness in the Presence of Death***. Shambhala, 2009, 204 pages, $16.95 paper bound.

"A traditional Tibetan saying tells us that if, on waking up in the morning, we do not meditate on death, the entire morning will be wasted. If we don't meditate on death at noon, the afternoon will be wasted. And if we don't meditate on death in the evening, the night will be lost to meaningless and frivolous pursuits."   page 185

Being With Dying is an intense book written with a balance of compassion and fearlessness that can best be described as fierce. Joan Halifax, PhD is an anthropologist, Zen priest, and Abbot of the Upaya Zen Center in Santa Fe, New Mexico. She has worked with dying people and their caregivers for over forty years. ***Being With Dying*** faces the mysteries of life and death with compassion, courage, equanimity, and wisdom. The orientation is Buddhist. The wisdom is universal.

The first time I read ***Being With Dying***, two sections had immediate impact: "to scour my heart out with honest sorrow" and "Do not squander your life."

"When my mother died, I received one of the hardest and most precious teachings of my entire life. I realized that I only had this one chance to grieve her death. I felt like I had a choice. On the one hand, I could be a so-called "good Buddhist," accept impermanent, and let go of my mother with great dignity. The other alternative was to scour my heart out with honest sorrow. I chose to scour."

page 192

"Life and death are of supreme importance
Time passes swiftly and opportunity is lost.
Let us awaken
     awaken...
Do not squander your life."

Zen Night Chant   page196

I adopted the concept and practice of scouring my heart out with honest sorrow even though my grieving processes can best be described as grieving on the installment plan. The need to scour one's heart out with honest sorrow is ancient wisdom. When reading the words "to scour my heart out with honest sorrow" I thought, "that is what I am doing and plan to continue for as long as I need." I identified with the "squandering" of my life and have been working to extend compassion and forgiveness to myself for straying from paths with heart and not always honoring my soul's purpose.

Being With Dying presents suggestions on facing death with courage, fearlessness, and equanimity as well as encountering death with compassion. Each chapter ends with a meditation to ground the topics presented in the chapter in an experience beyond words.

I highly recommend the meditation for encountering grief (page 195) which presents ten phrases to assist the cultivation of a tender heart and provides a concise summary of the practices of many wisdom traditions in encountering death.

"May I be open to the pain of grief.

May I find the inner resources to be present for my sorrow.

May I accept my sadness, knowing I am not my sadness.

May I accept my anger, fear, anxiety, and sorrow.

May I accept my grief, knowing that it does not make me bad or wrong.

May I forgive myself for not meeting my loved one's needs.

May I forgive myself for mistakes made and things left undone.

May I be open with myself and others about my experience of suffering.

May I find peace and strength that I may use my resources to help others.

May all who grieve be released from their sorrow."

I have read **Being With Death** multiple times during my bereavement and with each reading discover additional wisdom. **Being With Death** presents being in the presence of dying and death with fearless courage and a balance of complex compassion and equanimity. I must confess that equanimity alludes me. **Being With Death** is the most intense, most powerful, and most fierce of all the many books on loss and grief I have read. **Being With Death** is not an easy book to encounter but offers a treasure house of wisdom grounded in practice. Highly recommended.

111 Things That Help Grieving: **#89**

Book Resource 7

Dion Fortune. **Dion Fortune's Book of the Dead.** Weiser Books, 2005. First published in 1930 as **Through the Gates of Death**, 85 pages paper bound, $9.95.

Dion Fortune (1891-1946) was a powerful psychic who founded The Society of Light to further western mystery traditions. She wrote extensively about occultism, mysticism, and other esoteric mysteries. First published in 1930, **Through the Gates of Death** provides Dion Fortune's psychic insights about crossing the threshold and passing through the gates of death as well as offering comfort to those left behind. While the language may be a bit dated, the wisdom is universal and everlasting.

Dion Fortune on dreams:
"The Heaven-World appears familiar to the newcomer, and for this reason, we are all accustomed to go there in sleep every night! There is a sleep-life of the soul of which the average person is unaware because he does not bring back the memory upon waking. It is beyond the realm of dream, which is purely subconscious...It is the rousing of the soul to consciousness upon this plane which produces the dreams which are not like ordinary dreams..." page 14

Dion Fortune on telepathic communication:
"Let us always remember that if we can communicate telepathically during life, we shall have no difficulty in communication telepathically after death. For if minds can communicate without material means while both are upon earth, the position will not be materially affected when one of the pair has no longer got any material means wherewith to communicate but has to rely exclusively upon the mind." page 56

Dion Fortune on spirit communication:
"It may seem a strange thing to say, but true love is not emotional in its nature, but is an attitude of the soul towards life. True love is a spiritual radiation, like sunlight…It is true there must always be shock and emptiness when one upon whose love we have leant for years is taken from us, for the whole life must be readjusted…To those who are united in spirit, death is but a temporary severance. There must be loneliness, and there must be burdens to be shouldered alone that were once shared by the other, but there is not that sense of spiritual annihilation which devastates those who have laid up their treasure where moth and rust corrupt. It is this inner certainty of an enduring bond which is the sheet-anchor in times of bereavement….On the Inner Planes there is neither time or space as we understand it….When there is a real tuning of two souls, they are literally together on the Inner Planes, where to be of one mind is to be in one place….if there is a true spiritual union, we remain in touch, wherever our bodies may be…. If we

continue to love and be loved, even after the loss of the loved one, this spiritual widowing does not occur, and we are not left unmated. The intangible influence of the love continues to make itself felt…the bond of spiritual union survives all severance whether of space or time and continues to inspire and to protect both of those who are held in its tie, upon whatever plane they may be…This spiritual communion continues uninterruptedly through the death of the body and all the after death experiences of the soul….When spiritual love is coming to us from the Inner Planes we have only to still the outer senses for a moment to hear it purling like the brook, a steady flow, coming to us all the time from the eternal and steadfast soul that has gone on ahead to the Next Country. And we on our side, if we still love, may send out an equally steady flow to comfort our beloved." pages 24-26

Dion Fortune on black:
"The wearing of deep mourning has a very marked psychic effect. Black insulates the wearer from etheric vibrations, and a person so clad is more readily able to get in touch with the subtler planes that one clad in colours, which each attract their corresponding vibrations." pages 35-36

111 Things That Help Grieving: **#90**

Book Resource 8

Elizabeth Kubler-Ross and David Kessler. **On Grief and Grieving: Finding the Meaning of Grief Through the Five Stages of Loss**. Scribner, 2005, 235 pages paper bound, $16.00.

"...there is no pain greater than the loss of a loved one."   Elizabeth Kubler-Ross, page 214

Elizabeth Kubler-Ross's first book **On Death and Dying**, first published in 1969, describes five stages of dying: denial, anger, bargaining, depression, and acceptance. In her last book, **On Grief and Grieving**, written with David Kessler, the five stages of dying are applied to grief and grieving.

Regarding the five stages Kubler-Ross and Kessler write: "The stages have evolved since their introduction, and they have been very misunderstood over the past three decades. They were never meant to help tuck messy emotions into neat packages. They are responses to loss that many people have, but there is not a typical response to loss, as there is no typical loss. Our grief is as individual as our lives. The five stages…are a part of the framework that makes up our learning to live with the one we lost. They are tools to help us frame and identify what we may be feeling. But they are not stops on some linear timeline in grief. Not everyone goes through all of them or goes in a prescribed order."   page 7

"People often think of the stages as lasting weeks or months. They forget that the stages are responses to feelings that can last for minutes or hours as we flip in and out of one and then another. We do not enter and leave each individual stage in a linear fashion. We may feel one, then another, and back again to the first one." page 18

Denial: "Denial in grief has been misinterpreted over the years....For a person who has lost a loved one, however, the denial is more symbolic than literal....When we are in denial, we may respond at first by being paralyzed with shock or blanketed with numbness. The denial is still not *denial of the actual death*, even though someone may be saying, 'I can't believe he's dead.' The person is actually saying that, at first, because it is too much for his or her psyche." page 8

Anger: "This stage presents itself in many ways...Anger does not have to be logical or valid....The truth is that anger has no limits....Underneath anger is pain, *your* pain....Anger is strength and it can be an anchor, giving temporary structure to the nothingness of loss." pages 11-15

Bargaining: "Before a loss, it seems you will do anything if only your loved one may be spared....After a loss, bargaining may take the form of a temporary truce....'if only...' or 'What if...' statements....Guilt is often bargaining's companion....Bargaining can be an important reprieve from pain that occupies one's grief....Bargaining may fill the gaps that our strong emotions generally dominate, which often keep suffering at a distance." pages 17 and 19

Depression: "Empty feelings present themselves, and grief enters our lives on a deeper level, deeper than we ever imagined. This depressive stage feels as though it will last forever. It's important to understand that this depression is not a sign of mental illness. It is the appropriate response to a great loss. We withdraw from life, left in a fog of intense sadness, wondering, perhaps, if there is any point in going on alone. Why go on at all?...Depression after a loss is too often seen as unnatural: a state to be fixed, something to snap out of....But in grief, depression is a way for nature to keep us protected by shutting down the nervous system so that we can adapt to something we feel we cannot handle." pages 20-21

Acceptance: "Acceptance is often confused with the notion of being all right or okay with what has happened. This Is not the case. Most people don't ever feel okay or all right about the loss of a loved one. This stage is about accepting the reality that our loved one is physically gone and recognizing that this new reality is the permanent reality. We will never like this reality or make it okay, but eventually we accept it. We learn to live with it. It is the new norm with which we must learn to live....We must try to live now in a world where our loved one is missing....The more of your identity that was connected to your loved one, the harder it will be to do this." pages 24 and 25
"Acceptance is not about liking a situation. It is about acknowledging all that has been lost and learning to live with that loss....Acceptance is a process that we experience, not a final stage with an end point." pages 26 and 27

On Grief and Grieving presents the five stages of grief followed by a description of the inner world of grief and the outer world of grief. There is a section on specific circumstances of loss as well as the personal grief experiences of the authors.

On Closure: "No matter how you work at feeling your feelings fully, you never find the closure that you hear about or see in movies. But you do find a place for loss, a way to hold it and live with it….grief is not a project with a beginning and an end. It is a reflection of a loss that never goes away. We simply learn to live with it, both in the foreground and in the background. Where grief fits in our lives is an individual *thing*, often based on how far we have come in integrating the loss….Your don't ever bring the grief over a loved one to a close." page 158

"The reality is that you will grieve forever. You will not 'get over' the loss of a loved one; you will learn to live with it. You will heal, and you will rebuild yourself around the loss you have suffered. You will be whole again, but you will never be the same. Nor should you be the same, nor would you want to." page 230

On Afterlife: "Whatever the truth about life after death, we are certain that death does not exist as we imagine it. If you feel your loved one's presence, do not doubt it. They still exist….We are not suggesting that when you lose your loved one, you can skip the terrible pain of loss and separation, but we believe with all our hearts that even in death, our loved one still exists.   page 108

I highly recommend **On Grief and Grieving** as an excellent grief resource. The wisdom, compassion, and empathy transcends stages bringing healing words, concepts, and energy.

"I have loved and lost, and I am so much more than five stages. And so are you."
Elisabeth Kubler-Ross,   page 216

111 Things That Help Grieving: **#91**

Book Resource 9

Marie-Louise von Franz. **On Dreams and Death: A Jungian Interpretation.** Shambhala, 1987. Softcover, 193 pages. Currently out of print (available used).

On Dreams and Death: A Jungian Interpretation is a powerful book on the dreams of those nearing death and those who experience the death of a loved one. Marie-Louise von Franz primarily uses the symbolism of the Egyptian death ritual and alchemical symbolism to amplify archetypal death dreams. A valuable resource for understanding a Jungian approach to dream work specifically dreams involving death.

"It is in fact true, as Jung has emphasized, that the unconscious psyche pays very little attention to the abrupt end of bodily life and behaves as if the psychic life of the individual, that is the individuation process, will simply continue. In this connection, however, there are also dreams which symbolically indicate the end of bodily life and the explicit continuation of psychic life after death. The unconscious 'believes' quite obviously in a life after death.....The comforting message of the unconscious – that death is a 'cure' and that there is an afterlife – obviously cannot be interpreted here as a wish-fulfillment dream, for at the same time the end of physical existence is also predicted, quite brutally and unequivocally."   pages viii-ix

"A similar situation arises in the interpretation of those dreams wherein the dead appear to a still-living person. I will cite some of these in the following pages and interpret them as if they referred, on the objective level, to the postmortal life of the dead person (not to the life of the dreamer). I have had myself certain dreams which Jung interpreted in this way, which at the time was rather astonishing to me. He gave no reason for understanding precisely those dreams on the objective level; he usually interpreted such images on the subjective level, that is to say, as symbols of psychic contents to be found in the dreamer himself. I also was once asked by a woman analyst to study the dreams of a patient of hers, a young girl who had lost her fiancé, a pilot, in an airplane accident. She dreamed of the pilot almost every night, and the analyst and I at first interpreted the dream figure as the image of her own animus, which she had projected onto the fiancé. The unconscious seemed to be suggesting that she withdraw this projection and, by so doing, cure herself gradually of the 'loss of soul' suffered through the fiancé's death — that she detach herself from her tie with the dead. But there were six dreams which somehow I could not interpret in this manner. Therefore I told the analyst that in *those* dreams the appearance of the pilot was probably the dead man himself. The somewhat rationally inclined colleague was indignant, asked for a consultation with Jung and presented the whole dream series to him. Without hesitation, Jung (who knew nothing about my choice) picked out the same six dreams and interpreted them on the objective level. It seems to me that one can 'feel' whether the figure of a dead person in a dream is being used as a symbol for some inner reality or whether it 'really' represents the dead. It is difficult, however, to set up universally valid criteria for this 'feeling.' At best it can be said that if the interpretation on the subjective level makes little or no sense, even though the dream has an especially strong numinous effect, then interpretation on the objective level might be taken into consideration." page xv

"Edinger calls the series of dreams in **Ego and Archetype** 'metaphysical' dreams. They are indeed different from the majority of dreams we work with in psychotherapeutic practice. Somehow they cannot be interpreted very well on the subjective level, that is, as symbolic representations of subjective inner processes. This means that they cannot, in Jung's terminology, be 'psychologized.' One feels compelled to leave them in space as a symbolic statement about another reality from which we are separated by a mysterious and dangerous barrier." pages 156-157

Review by Elisabeth Kubler-Ross:
"Marie-Louise von Franz has to be congratulated on a true masterpiece of research and interpretations of dreams by patients prior to a sudden or anticipated death. The common denominator does not seem to be simply an end of earthly existence, but transformation into a continuation of another form of life. Although

there exists ever-increasing literature on the topic of death, very little has been studied and published on the content and meaning of unconscious material of these individuals. Since most of us 'thanatologists' have focused on the care and preparation of the individual and the assistance of the caregivers, much work is needed for those who are more interested in the in-depth study of these patients, who can become our teachers as well. **On Dreams and Death** is a fantastic book, full of the wisdom and insight which only a Jungian like Marie-Louise von Franz can write. It gives one a deeper respect for our inner knowledge, for the deep significance of dreams, and last but not least, for ancient and present customs whose origin we have long forgotten! Thank you for sharing this significant contribution to the psychology and understanding of dreaming and death." back cover

111 Things That Help Grieving: **#92**

Book Resource 10

T.J. Wray and Ann Back Price. **Grief Dreams: How They Help Heal Us After the Death of a Loved One.** Jossey-Bass, 2005, 211 pages soft cover, $26.00.

Grief Dreams presents the concept that grief dreams are healing. "Because grief dreams are a fairly universal phenomenon among the bereaved, they offer the opportunity, when affirmed as important and properly understood, for healing….Grief dreams allow us to reconnect with our loved ones, to return to that place where nothing has changed – a place where our loved one is still alive – a place where grief does not exist. In one incredible, magical moment, the chasm of death and despair evaporate, and we are given a few precious moments with our beloved. And here in lies the amazing power of the *grief dream*."

pages 1 and 2

Wray and Price present four major categories of grief dreams: visitation, message, reassurance and trauma dreams. They note that types of grief dreams can be combined in one dream as well as other types of grief dreams including intentional, lucid, series, prophetic, and day dreams. A chapter is devoted to each of the four major categories and examples are presented followed by a presentation of the dreamer's background story, an analysis of the dream, how the dream works to provide healing for the dreamer, and how the dream may be of help to the reader. A chapter is devoted to faith and grief dreams and the book ends with a chapter summarizing how grief dreams help with healing. The appendices include lists of reader resources and selected references.

Grief Dreams is a helpful resource, particularly if you have little to no experience with dream work. The authors do not directly address what Marie-Louise von Franz and C.G. Jung term "objective dreams," however, they imply, through the dream examples selected, that grief dreams involving visits by a disembodied loved one are not "subjective dreams."

Note: See book resource 9 (#91, page 234) for summary information regarding Marie-Louise von Franz's book **On Dreams and Death** (1984). Other helpful dream resources include **The Way of the Dream: Conversations on Jungian Dream Interpretation with Marie-Louise von Franz** by Fraser Boa (1988) and Jeremy Taylor **The Wisdom of Your Dreams: Using Dreams to Tap into Your Unconscious and Transform Your Life** (2009).

111 Things That Help Grieving: #93

Book Resource 11

Susan A. Berger. **The Five Ways We Grieve: Finding Your Personal Path to Healing after the Loss of a Loved One.** Trumpeter Books/Shambhala, 2009, 223 pages, $26.95 hardbound.

Susan Berger is a licensed clinical social worker who interviewed sixty people to determine the long term impact of loss. For those she interviewed she established a minimum period of five years since the loss. The five ways or types of grieving were identified from the interviews.

The first type she calls **nomads** who are described as not dealing with their grief or the impact of their loss on their lives. **Memorialists** create memorials and rituals to preserve and honor the memory of their loved ones. **Normalizers** actively create or re-create a sense of family and community. **Activists** focus on helping others dealing with the same disease or issues that caused the death of their loved one. **Seekers** search for meaning through religious, philosophical, or spiritual beliefs and practices. Each of the five types is described in detail with examples and a section of the advantages and disadvantages of each type. Each chapter closes with strategies for healing and growth, questions for further exploration, and reflections for each type. Susan Berger found the largest number of the people she interviewed fit into the normalizer type, around one-third were memorialists, and twenty percent were activists. She noted that around fifteen percent evidenced complicated grief leading to a "long term nomad" type.

Regarding seekers she notes, "Seekers experience the death of a loved one as a catalyst for exploring the spiritual questions about life....Their focus is on exploring the spiritual, the sacred, and the divine."

page 135

"Of the five identified types, seekers may be considered unconventional in American society. Whether it is the commitment they make to connecting with a community of believers or the intensity with which they embrace their spiritual nature, the seekers' search for something beyond themselves is a quest for connection with the divine and its manifestation in them."

pages 153-154

It seems likely that if you are reading **111 Things That Help Grieving** you are probably a seeker as your primary type. Susan Berger indicates that while one type is primary for each person she interviewed the primary type can change over time. In my experience, one may have a primary type of approach to grieving but that does not exclude other types as secondary ways of grieving.

The five types, ways, or styles of grieving provide increased awareness of how individuals cope, adjust, and deal with the loss of a loved one. The different types may not be fully compatible and lead to tension, conflict, and misunderstandings between family members, friends, and associates.

Susan Berger has provided a frame work that is not based on stages of grief but types or styles of grieving that offers improved awareness, understanding, and compassion.

111 Things That Help Grieving: **#94**

Book Resource 12

Brook Noel and Pamela D. Blair. **I Wasn't Ready To Say Goodbye: Surviving, Coping, and Healing After the Sudden Death of a Loved One.** Sourcebooks, 2000/2008, 292 pages, $15.99 paper bound.

"On October 4, 1997, I acquired a pair of grief-colored glasses without a choice of whether to accept them or not. In the years to follow I would learn owning a pair is life's greatest responsibility, heaviest weight, and potentially a gift – if one can adjust them and learn how to focus in spite of them. I have worn glasses all my life; glasses that helped me see what I *wanted* to see more clearly and *corrected* my vision to that of the average person. My grief-colored glasses have no resemblance to the glasses I have known before. At first they were a massive blur from my tears. I could see only the inch in front of me, and I struggled to find something to steady myself. I ached to remove them, break them, send them back, but that was impossible then – and still is today. I own them for life." page 254
Brook Noel, July 29, 2007

I Wasn't Ready To Say Goodbye is a heartfelt, practical, and resource rich book written by two women who experienced the sudden loss of a loved one and collaborated to tell their stories, the stories of others, and provide resources they discovered along the way. Despite the subtitle about "sudden death" the book is an excellent resource about coping with loss and grief even if your loved one did not die suddenly. While dying may be protracted, the moment of death is sudden for us all. Most of us are not ready to say goodbye and experience life made so much more complex by the disembodiment of our loved ones.

The book starts with a section of practical advice for the first few weeks of bereavement. The section then describes the emotional and physical effects of grief as well as myths and misunderstandings about the grieving process. The twenty-eight myths provide practical suggestions to living in a grief adverse culture where loss is compounded by avoidance and denial. The second major section focuses on the intense disruption created by loss, including relating to others, difficult days, gender differences in grieving, and children and grief. Part three presents loss by different types of relationships (parent, child, spouse, sibling, others) and presents specific information about each. Part four is called "pathways through grief" which includes information about the grief journey, faith, self-help and therapy, and grief recovery and exercises. The book also contains appendixes of grief resources and other support information.

If you have not read **I Wasn't Ready To Say Goodbye**, I encourage you to do so no matter where you might be on your grief pathway. The book is an excellent resource providing practical advice from the heart.

111 Things That Help Grieving: **#95**

Book Resource 13

Michael Newton. **Journey of Souls: Case Studies of Life Between Lives**. Llewellyn, 1994, 278 pages, $16.95 paper bound.

Michael Newton, PhD; a counseling psychologist and master hypnotherapist; while providing past life regression therapy discovered hypnotized individuals could describe their life between lives. **Journey of Souls** presents the experiences of twenty-nine people, during the period between lives, when their disembodied soul resided in the spirit realm. The book describes death and departure, gateway to the spirit realm, homecoming, orientation, transition, placement, and spirit realm guides, as seen by the hypnotized individuals from the perspective of their disembodied souls. The book summarizes levels of souls and the progression leading to rebirth.

In 2000, Michael Newton published **Destiny of Souls: New Case Studies of Life Between Lives** expanding the information presented in his first book with sixty-seven additional cases. **Destiny of Souls** describes the spirit world in greater detail including earthly spirits, spiritual energy restoration, soul groups, council of elders, community dynamics including soulmates, and the advanced soul. (**Destiny of Souls**, Llewellyn, 2000, 409 pages, $17.05 paper bound).

In 2004, Michael Newton published a manual for practitioners of life between lives hypnotherapy. While the book's primary focus is as a training manual for the Michael Newton Institute for Life Between Lives Hypnotherapy, the book further amplifies the information about spirit realm existence between lives. (**Life Between Lives: Hypnotherapy for Spiritual Regression**, Llewellyn, 2004, 222 pages, $15.95 paper bound.)

Memories of the Afterlife: Life Between Lives: Stories of Personal Transformation, Edited by Michael Newton was published in 2009 (Llewellyn, 310 pages, $17.95 paper bound) presents thirty two case studies of life between lives hypnosis sessions written by members of the Newton Institute.

I found the information presented in the life between lives books to be compelling, comforting, and compatible with my own experiences in the altered state I call golden dreams. Should you be inspired to read one of Michael Newton's books, I recommend starting with the first book, **Journey of Souls**, as it provides the foundation which is expanded in the later books.

111 Things That Help Grieving: **#96**

Book Resource 14

Alan D. Wolfelt. **Healing A Spouse's Grieving Heart: 100 Practical Ideas After Your Husband Or Wife Dies: Compassionate Advice and Simple Activities for Widows and Widowers**. Companion Press, 2003, 111 pages, $11.95 paper bound.

"The death of a spouse tears through every layer of your existence. It will take time and hard work to sew up those many tears, and even then the 'repairs' will always be a part of who you are. Healing does not mean forgetting or 'getting over.' In fact, that is no such thing as 'getting over' grief. That term is the cruelest of fallacies. You don't 'get over' grief. You learn to live with it. You learn to accommodate it and make it part of who you are. But if you mourn well, over time and with the support of others, your grief will soften. No, it will never end, and it is likely that a day won't go by that you don't think about and miss your precious husband or wife. But, your grief will become less sharp and all-consuming. It will take on the blurred, bittersweet qualities of memory. On most days, it will murmur gently in the background while in the foreground, your life proceeds with meaning and purpose."

> from the Introduction, pages 2 and 3

Alan Wolfelt, PhD is a grief counselor and Director of The Center for Loss and Life Transition in Fort Collins, Colorado. **Healing A Spouse's Grieving**

Heart provides one hundred ideas, concepts, and activities across a wide range of topics related to the loss of a spouse and the experiences of bereavement. The one hundred ideas and concepts are presented one per page with a suggested activity for each topic. As suggested by the subtitles, Alan Wolfelt provides advice that is both practical and compassionate. The book is written in a clear and easily understood style summarizing the discoveries he made during his years of grief counseling.

Healing A Spouse's Grieving Heart is an excellent grief resource book to read early in bereavement when searching for practical suggestions for coping with the loss of a beloved spouse. The book is also a valuable resource to those whose bereavement is measured in years not weeks or months.

111 Things That Help Grieving: **#97**

Book Resource 15

Alberto Villoldo. **Shaman, Healer, Sage: How To Heal Yourself and Others with the Energy Medicine of the Americas**, Random House, 2000, 243 pages, $24.00 hardcover.

Alberto Villoldo, PhD, is a medical anthropologist who trained with Inka shamans of the Andes and the Amazon for twenty-five years. In **Shaman, Healer, Sage** he presents a distilled summary of his training. Major concepts are the luminous energy field and the illumination process of healing.

"True healing is nothing less than an awakening to a vision of our healed nature and the experience of infinity." page 10

Alberto Villoldo was initiated into the major rites of Andean shaman and has adapted these sacred rites with the blessings of his teachers who intended for him to offer them to any and all interested persons. The rites are called the Munay-Ki rites and can be reviewed at munay-ki.org.

"The Amazon shamans believe that when you clear all your chakras you acquire a 'rainbow body.'...According to legend, when you acquire the rainbow body you can make the journey beyond death to the Spirit World." page 73

The process of healing our luminous energy field is described through the illumination process and through cleansing our chakras.

In addition to the Munay-Ki rites, Alberto Villoldo has established a training program called the Healing the Light Body School. More information is available at thefourwinds.com.

Alberto Villoldo's latest two books; **A Shaman's Miraculous Tools for Healing**, 2015 and **One Spirit Medicine,** 2015 are briefly described as book resources 16 and 17 (#98 and #99).

Also recommended are the following books by Alberto Villoldo:

Mending the Past and Healing the Future with Soul Retrieval, 2005.

The Four Insights: Wisdom, Power, and Grace of the Earthkeepers, 2006.

Courageous Dreaming: How Shamans Dream the World Into Being, 2008.

Illumination: The Shaman's Way of Healing, 2010.

Power Up Your Brain: The Neuroscience of Enlightment, 2011, David Perlmutter, MD and Alberto Villoldo, PhD.

111 Things That Help Grieving: **#98**

Book Resource 16

Alberto Villoldo with Anne E. O'Neill. **A Shaman's Miraculous Tools for Healing**. Hampton Roads, 2015, 235 pages, $18.95 soft cover.

A Shaman's Miraculous Tools for Healing (2015) is an excellent companion to the book **Shaman, Healer, Sage** (2000). In **Shaman, Healer, Sage** Alberto Villoldo presents his translation of the healing work of the shaman of the Amazon and Andes. In the new companion book each major aspect of the healing work is presented in the voices of his clients and includes the healer's reflections. The book provides an intimate glimpse into the healing experiences of twelve of his clients providing the practical application of the concepts of **Shaman, Healer, Sage**.

I recommend reading **Shaman, Healer, Sage** first followed by **A Shaman's Miraculous Tools for Healing** as the first provides the concepts of the healing traditions of the shaman and the second offers examples of the application of the healing traditions in the voices of his clients.

Should the healing traditions practiced by Alberto Villoldo appeal to you, may you have the good fortune of locating an energy healer trained by Alberto Villoldo's school. See The Four Winds Society and Light Body Energy Medicine School for additional information.

111 Things That Help Grieving: **#99**

Book Resource 17

Alberto Villoldo. **One Spirit Medicine: Ancient Ways to Ultimate Wellness.** Hay House, 2015, 209 pages, $24.99 hard cover.

In **One Spirit Medicine,** Alberto Villoldo describes the healing traditions of the shaman of the Amazon and Andes as well as the healing traditions of medical doctors Mark Hyman, MD, **The Blood Sugar Solution** (2012) and David Perlmutter, MD, and Alberto Villoldo, PhD, **Power Up Your Brain: The Neuroscience of Enlightenment** (2011). He describes his personal healing experiences using the healing wisdom of the shaman and the medical knowledge of his two physicians. **One Spirit Medicine** summarizes his life's work practicing the healing traditions of shaman integrated with advances in western medical practices.

The second half of the book is devoted to a description of the medicine wheel as a map for the healing challenges at each of the four directions using archetypal mythology as examples to illustrate each of the cardinal points. The last chapter describes the vision quest as a way to actualize the recommendations presented in **One Spirit Medicine** by putting the concepts and ideas into practice.

One Spirit Medicine is an excellent resource providing the wisdom of ancient healing traditions of shaman of the Amazon and Andes blended with modern western medicine as represented by the cutting edge medical science of Drs. Hyman and Perlmutter.

111 Things That Help Grieving: **#100**

Book Resource 18

Dennis William Hauck. **The Emerald Tablet: Alchemy for Personal Transformation**. Penguin, 1999, 454 pages, $16.95 soft cover.

The Emerald Tablet: Alchemy for Personal Transformation by Dennis William Hauck provides an excellent introduction to alchemy with a focus on the Emerald Tablet, an ancient text written on an emerald crystal. The creator of the Emerald Tablet is unknown; however, the Emerald Tablet has been attributed to Thoth, an Egyptian god, and Hermes, a Greek god. The Emerald Tablet is said to contain the secrets of alchemy.

Dennis William Hauck describes the Emerald Tablet and its influence throughout history, as well as interpretations of the symbolism and meanings of the images of the Emerald Tablet.

The second section of the book provides a seven step application of the processes of the Emerald Tablet, how each of the alchemical processes have been applied historically, and how each can be applied by an individual in their personal alchemical process of purification and transformation. A separate chapter is devoted to each of the seven steps or processes of alchemy.

The Emerald Tablet provides a balanced presentation of alchemy from physical, psychological, and metaphysical perspectives that balances interior alchemical experiences with exterior alchemical experiences and the above with the below.

Dennis William Hauck has written other books about alchemy including **Sorcerer's Stone: A Beginner's Guide to Alchemy** which links alchemy with the planets and their associated metals in relation to the seven operations described by the Emerald Tablet.

The Emerald Tablet is not a bereavement book but is recommended as the loss of a loved one produces an intense psychological alchemical environment that may lead to the alchemy of transformation. The images of alchemy provide powerful descriptions of the grieving process as well as suggesting potential ways of healing and transformation.

111 Things That Help Grieving

"...the fire has to burn the fire, one just has to burn in the emotion till the fire dies down and becomes balanced....which unfortunately cannot be evaded. The burning of the fire, of the emotion, cannot not be tricked out of one's system; there is no recipe for getting rid of it, it has to be endured. The fire has to burn until the last unclean element has been consumed... It cannot be hindered but only suffered till what is mortal or corruptible... has been burnt up. That is the meaning, it is the acceptance of suffering. ...Sitting in Hell and roasting there is what brings forth the philosopher's stone..."

Marie-Louise von Franz

Section Five

Alchemy of the Heart

Section five uses the images, language, and concepts of alchemy in a feeble attempt to comprehend the mysteries of **love** – the radiant gold of abundance in great measure and **loss** – the black lead of abundance in great measure with the abundance being **grief** and the experience of the hellfires of grief and black nights of the soul. The mysteries of **transformation** are explored using alchemical processes to describe a small golden flame in the midst of the black fires of grief. One of the final mysteries hidden within the hellfires of grief is **eternal love** – abundance beyond measure. Alchemy of the heart describes love loss grief transformation eternal love swirling in the heart of hearts of the embodied soul whose loved one has disembodied.

111 Things That Help Grieving: **#101**

Alchemy: Concepts & Images

I have been fascinated with alchemical concepts and images for as long as I can remember. With the disembodiment of my soulmate the concepts and images of alchemy assumed an even more prominent role in my efforts to cope, adjust, and slowly start the transformational process towards regaining my equilibrium. Alchemy, in the primary stages, (the lesser work) is concerned with refining, purification, and extracting the essences of minerals, chemicals, plants, and/or human beings. The focus of later stages (the greater work) is the transformation leading to the realization of quientessenses, and the transmutation from lead to gold. The lead of human beings, when speaking in an appreciative manner, are the unrealized potentials of the person. The transformation in psychological language is the self actualization process (Maslow) or the individuation process (Jung). In the midst of the hellfires of grief these intellectual thoughts offer little to no comfort. The processes, concepts, and images of alchemy speak a symbolic language that transcends rational thought and provides nourishment to one's embodied soul at a time when nourishment is sorely lacking and intensely needed.

The phases, steps, stages, images, concepts, and processes of alchemy have provided me with a crude roadmap of at least some of the landscape of the hellfires of grief which holds the possibility of being transformed by the alchemy of grief like the phoenix who survives the fires to be reborn. The images of alchemy may not resonate or have energy for your logical conscious mind, but their power, wisdom, and truth are clearly communicated at a level both above and below rational thought and most feeling states. One classic alchemical book consists of fifteen illustrations with no words. The book called **Liber Mutus** (Mute Book) "speaks" a language all can understand if enough energy is applied to the process. In the **Liber Mutus,** the illustrations are divided into a lower level and upper level – the above and below in alchemical language which can be converted to the physical realm (below) and spirit realm (above). It is reported that understanding and conducting the operations illustrated in the **Liber Mutus** will enable the practitioners to purify, transform, and realize their essences or true nature and open the channel to follow the soul's work.

Should the alchemical things that help grieving have little to no interest or energy for you please skip them and hopefully you will find some of the other things that help grieving to contain useful information. Perhaps the alchemical concepts, images, stages, phases, and processes will provide you with comfort, solace, and perhaps the faintest glimpse of the gold that is obscured by the black lead of grief.

Adam McLean. **A Commentary on the Mutus Liber: Magnum Opus Hermetic Sourceworks #11**, Phanes Press, 1991.

111 Things That Help Grieving: **#102**

Alchemy: Processes & Operations

"In my opinion it is quite hopeless to try to establish any kind of order in the infinite chaos of substances and procedures." *
                    C.G. Jung. **Psychology and Alchemy**

The alchemical literature describes numerous steps, stages, processes, and operations of alchemy. Alchemical processes and operations are often separated into three phases – the black phase, white phase, and the red or purple phase. The black phase includes calcination (fire), dissolution (water), separation (air), conjunction (earth), and the early phases of fermentation (called putrefaction). In the second phase of fermentation, the black phase, transforms separating the black into the birth of something new which Western alchemists call the peacock's tail and Eastern alchemists call the golden pill or golden elixir. In the white phase, the product of fermentation is distilled repeatedly until the quintessence is realized. In the red or purple phase, the result of successful distillation produces a coagulation which alchemists call the child of conjunction or the philosopher's stone. Although not often mentioned, the higher level stages move beyond purification and transformation to transmutation. In transmutation the lead of the black phase is changed into gold.

Alchemical processes occur at all levels including physical, mental, emotional, social, soul, and spirit levels. As C.G. Jung clearly states, the processes of alchemy are chaotic with attempts to separate into stages or steps being arbitrary. Since it is the nature of human beings to establish or inscribe order to provide some degree of control (real or imagined), alchemists (following the guidance provided by the emerald tablet) have traditionally identified seven major stages and three phases of alchemical operations. In practice or experience the stages, steps, and/or phases overlap, merge, and occur simultaneously. Alchemists have separated, isolated, and labeled the various aspects of chaos in order to better understand the processes of nature and to assist or expedite the process. While clearly arbitrary, the wisdom of alchemy applied to grief and grieving may provide value in transforming the black lead of grief by separating the black lead from the golden rainbow energy of love and with good fortune beyond measure, transmuting the golden love into eternal or celestial love.

The following alchemical things that help grieving employ the traditional seven stages or processes most commonly described in the alchemical literature. It is important to remember that just like the stages described in the grief literature, the stages of alchemy are not rigid, distinct, or discrete stages, but overlap, merge, and occur simultaneously. Traditionally, alchemical procedures involving physical substances are of extreme duration with the preparation of various compounds taking many months to many years to refine and combine. Alchemical transformation and transmutation of the alchemist is a lifelong quest to produce the philosopher's stone (West) or the golden pill or elixir of immortality (East).

---

*C.G. Jung. **Psychology and Alchemy**: Collected Works Volume 12, Second Edition, Princeton University Press, 1968, page 288.

111 Things That Help Grieving: **#103**

Alchemy of Love/Alchemy of Loss

In the alchemy of love connections are made between two people. The more intense the love the greater are the number of connections established. Connections are not limited to the physical realm, as subtle spirit realm connections are included. The connections include energy centers and if you are fortunate beyond measure to rediscover your soulmate the connections include soul and spirit level connections. Connections are made at the level of each chakra and each energy body.

In alchemical terms, the relationship will include experiencing the rough edges of one another as well as experiencing the full range and intensity of emotions. Burning in the emotional crucible of the relationship forges additional and stronger connections, as the lead of unrealized potential is transformed by the intense experience of burning (calcination). The intense emotional flooding (including tears) dissolves old ways, transforming both partners (dissolution). The burning and flooding result in the identification of the essences of both persons; at the level of soul and spirit; separated from those aspects of each that are not part of one's higher nature (separation). The separated essences are then combined in what alchemists call the sacred marriage (sun and moon, king and queen) (conjunction). These alchemical processed take place both within each person as well as between the partners. The sacred marriage is subjected to further calcination, dissolution, separation, and conjunction in the process alchemists term fermentation. The process of fermentation is also referred to as the dark night of the soul that hopefully results in a transformational experience that improves awareness providing inspiration from the spirit realm. The products of fermentation are separated, refined, and purified by the process of distillation where they are heated by the combined energies of the partners. The golden rainbow cocoon or energy field, formed during the process of conjunction, is further refined and fused with spirit during the phase of coagulation as the quintessences produced during distillation are combined resulting in a transformation that transmutes the dichotomy of above and below (spirit realm and physical realm) as the partners realize the nature of their celestial love.

The alchemical processes described above can be applied to all energy transactions and transformations. With the disembodiment of one of the partners the alchemy of love transforms into the alchemy of loss. With the disembodiment of one of the partners, the physical connections are severed resulting in intense trauma. The lower chakra cords are severed between the two, resulting in a hemorrhaging of energy of the partner who remains embodied. The chakra cords flail about looking to reconnect. The resulting rawness, chaos, and despair I have referred to as experiencing the hellfires of grief. The hellfires of grief are not common fire rather they are subtle fire, invisible to physical eyes, burn without destroying, and are intensely hot without producing physical heat. The heartfires of love continue but have been overwhelmed or eclipsed by the hellfires of grief. Each of the alchemical processes applied to loss will be described in separate things that help grieving sections. Briefly the hellfires of grief correspond to calcination. The intense emotional flooding, including tears, corresponds to dissolution. The process of separation is a painful process including one's life review reliving memories both good and bad, often with an emphasis on regrets and remorse. Eventually the life review process produces improved awareness at the levels of soul and spirit. The conjunction process takes place at the level of the heart where thoughts are balanced by feelings and intuition prevails. In order for the alchemy of loss to progress towards transformation, conjunction must talk place within the heart of hearts. This subtle chamber is not a physical realm structure rather the abode of the embodied soul. The intense experience of loss ferments in the heart of hearts which has been broken open by the loss. Over time and with an open heart, the fermentation process results in improved awareness of the essences, and eventually with good fortune beyond measure, to the transformation of the essences to their quintessences. The distillation process opens the way to the spirit realm and the awareness of celestial or spirit love. I can only speculate about these later phases (distillation and coagulation) as I continue to be mired in the earlier stages with only glimpses of the golden rainbow dragon energies of the spirit realm. In coagulation the transformation moves beyond opposites until polarity is transmuted into the spirit realm of eternal love. The black lead of loss is transmuted into the gold of eternal love. Of course I am only speculating but I have experienced brief glimpses in golden dreams, inspirations, and other messages.

111 Things That Help Grieving: **#104**

Calcination (Fire): Alchemy

"'He extinguishes the fire in its own inner measure.'...the fire has to burn the fire, one just has to burn in the emotion till the fire dies down and becomes balanced. That is something which unfortunately cannot be evaded. The burning of the fire, of the emotion, cannot not be tricked out of one's system; there is no recipe for getting rid of it, it has to be endured. The fire has to burn until the last unclean element has been consumed, which is what all alchemical texts say in different variations, and we have not found any other way either. It cannot be hindered but only suffered till what is mortal or corruptible, or as our text says so beautifully, till the corruptible humidity, the unconsciousness, has been burnt up. That is the meaning, it is the acceptance of suffering. ...Sitting in Hell and roasting there is what brings forth the philosopher's stone; as it is said here, the fire is extinguished with its own inner measure."*

Marie-Louise von Franz

The hellfires of grief are not elementary or common physical fire. Common or physical fire is visible, creates heat, consumes or destroys the fuel, and stops when the fuel is depleted. In addition to gross physical or common fire, alchemists describe three other types of fire. Central fire is the energy of objects, secrete fire is the fire of the life force or soul, and celestial fire is the fire of spirit. The subtle fires are not visible with the physical senses, burn without producing physical heat, do not destroy the vessel in which they are burning, and do not destroy the object. The hellfires of grief is a type of flame that is invisible to physical senses. Hellfires of grief are experienced as intensely hot, yet no physical heat is generated, burn without consuming, and in my personal experience appear to be inexhaustible. Hellfires of grief express the intense emotions that result from the disembodiment of a loved one.

In alchemical images, the black hellfires of grief are fueled by the emotions of grief, as well as the negative aspects of regrets and remorse. The hellfires of grief burn the lead of regrets and remorse in an attempt to purify and transcend the black lead converting the darkness of loss into the white light of love. Initially the hellfires of grief burn the black lead of regrets and remorse, purifying the lead of loss, which results not in an immediate transformation to white, but a gradual refinement, where the black lead slowly transforms to pure lead minus the black impurities. The resulting pure lead is then ready to experience higher levels and more subtle transformations. This process is not measured in weeks or months but in years and years. In psychological language, the process is that of a life review where all of the experiences are reviewed, processed, and if successful, transformed to a level less contaminated by the black lead of regrets, remorse, guilt, and shame. The continually burning subtle fire eventually produces glimpses of the golden light of the celestial or spirit realm fires of eternal love.

The hellfires of grief, while intensely painful, are necessary to remove the black dross or impurities of one's negative thinking; to reduce the experience of loss to its intensely painful reality without the added burdens of regrets, remorse, guilt, shame, and resulting despair. Pure loss is more than painful enough without the excessive baggage of the experience of ruminations about ones faults and failings. The hellfires of grief burn the errors of omission and errors of commission in an intensely painful and protracted process over years and years. As Marie-Louise von Franz so eloquently expresses it there is no other way.

The alchemical process of calcination is not an isolated process as the hellfires of grief are also accompanied by the process of dissolution (water).

---

*Marie-Louise von Franz. **Alchemy: An Introduction to the Symbolism and the Psychology.** Inner City Books, 1980, pages 252 and 254.

111 Things That Help Grieving: **#105**

Dissolution (Water): Alchemy

Dissolution is the process of adding water or another liquid to the remains of calcination. In the alchemy of grief, dissolution takes the form of tears, crying, and other emotional flooding. Letting go, experiencing, and expressing intense, often contradictory, emotions. The process of dissolution often overwhelms the usual ways of coping leaving the person feeling psychologically naked and vulnerable as the usual coping strategies either do not work or have limited effectiveness. The intense hellfires of grief are blended with the soul's tears in an intense experience of fire and water that merges, blends, and repeats over and over. The emotional flooding includes an intense mix of anger, sadness, helplessness and hopelessness, powerlessness, despair, regrets and remorse, guilt, shame, and others. I have described the experience as being struck by invisible black lightning during a violent storm.

In describing the work (opus) of alchemy, Marie-Louise von Franz states "...the first activity of the opus is distilling, washing, and cleaning, over and over again. Here it says nine times, others say fifteen times, and some say ten years. It is really a very long process and some times means endless rehearsing the same problem in its different aspects. That is why also in alchemical texts they always allude to the fact that this part can go on for a very long time and is characterized by endless repetitions...."*

        Marie-Louise von Franz

The repeated burning (calcination) and washing (dissolution) of the raw materials of grief will take place with or without conscience participitation. Alchemists work with processes found in nature and attempt to expedite, enhance, and assist the transformation from the black raw material (black lead of grief) to extract the essence (underlying golden love) and, with further work to transmute the essence (love) into its quintessence (spirit, celestial, or eternal love). The early phases of grief focus mostly on the transformation of the black lead of loss to realize the underlying essence of love. Both calcination and dissolution are part of the alchemical black phase. It is important to realize and remember that these two processes coexist and, along with the process of separation, continues for years. The process of purification and refinement slowly transforms, making possible greater access to more subtle levels. This work is more at the level of mind and soul with later alchemical processes being at more subtle levels involving soul and spirit.

In psychological terms, the person is nearly overwhelmed and all but drowned in the experience of the hellfires of grief and its flood of emotions. Rational thinking no longer prevails seeming grossly inadequate and hopeless naive. Long held priorities lose power and seem silly, even stupid. The hellfires of grief and dissolution may create an intense crisis of values and purpose. While perhaps not the optimal time to conduct a life review, the loss may lead to self-inquiry about one's life, purpose, and meaning. The overwhelming question that underlies much of the questing is the why of death, specifically the death of one's beloved, as well as larger existential questions about life and death. Of course not everyone embraces (either willingly or by default) these existential struggles. If you are reading this section on the alchemy of grieving, you likely have the need to transform your loss and; if blessed with good fortune beyond measure; transmute your loss by increasing your subtle spirit realm awareness.

*Marie-Louise von Franz. **Alchemy: An Introduction to the Symbolism and the Psychology.** Inner City Books, 1980, pages 221-222.

111 Things That Help Grieving: **#106**

Separation (Air): Alchemy

"Separate the earth from fire, the subtle from the gross, gently and with great ingenuity."*
> **The Emerald Tablet**
> translated by Dennis William Hauck

The alchemical process of separation applied to the alchemy of grieving is part of the life review process, separating good memories from bad memories, loving acts from non-loving acts, loving words from non-loving words, regrets and remorse from loving acts, words and thoughts. The darker aspects are purified in the hellfires of grief and further refined in the flooding of dissolution constitute the essential aspects (essences) to be embraced while the dark, black dregs resulting from the operations of fire and water are discarded ,as they are no longer relevant. The process of separation is repeated over and over until only pure essences remain. Of course this is conjecture on my part since my burning and flooding alchemical operations are far from completed.

The process of separation begins the dawning awareness of the essences of soul and spirit. In alchemical operations, separation can take many forms from simple evaporation to filtration to simple distillation to fractional vacuum distillation. In the alchemy of grief the process of separation may begin in the head (mind) but the real alchemy takes place in the crucible of the heart. The crucible of the heart is the location of the essential alchemical operations of grieving. The hellfires of grief, soul's tears, emotional flooding, and operations of separation all take place within the heart of hearts.

In alchemical operations the raw materials are refined by fire and water then subjected to separation by air into the essences (which rise) and the dregs (which fall) to be subjected to additional purification. In the alchemy of grief the operations are applied to the raw materials of grief by repeated burning in the hellfire of grief and flooding in the emotions of grief until the black lead of grief is cleansed and purified of impurities which raise vibrational levels allowing for more subtle alchemical operations to proceed.

*Dennis William Hauck. **The Emerald Tablet: Alchemy for Personal Transformation**. Penguin, 1999, page 45.

111 Things That Help Grieving: **#107**

Conjunction (Earth): Alchemy

"It rises from earth to heaven and descends again to earth, thereby combining within itself the powers of the Above and the Below."*
>	**The Emerald Tablet**
>	translated by Dennis William Hauck

The alchemical process of conjunction brings together the elements separated and saved during the burning, washing, and separation processes. The process of conjunction brings the products of fire, water, and air together grounding them so they might join. Conjunction is the joining of essences that have been purified by the earlier operations.

In the experience of grief, logic and rationality become overwhelmed by the hellfires of grief, flood of emotions, and separation of outdated values, priorities, and goals. With the loss of a loved one, the over valuation of logical rational three dimensional thinking is corrected by an intensification of feeling states and emotional ways of being. This process is usually not within conscious control and feels like being attacked by emotions that are beyond control. Intuition may be strengthened or discovered if previously dormant. A broken heart is an open heart and more receptive to the experience of the subtle spirit realm and dimensions beyond the limits of logical rational thinking which include feelings, images, symbols, and other non-linear ways of knowing. The merger of previously separate aspects (traditional stereotyped male and female aspects) provides for more complete and balanced functioning. However, the experience is not one of appreciation, as the scrambling of ones being is an intense experience of chaos in the hellfires of grief, dark nights of the soul, and flooding of emotions. For some the discovery of the other, often unexpressed, side of one's human nature further complicates the grieving process as logic and rational thought are no match for the hellfires of grief, emotional flooding, or the purification process, and discovery of our more pure true nature (essences).

The readjustment after a loss involve alchemical processes that provide the energy to develop different values, different purposes, different priorities with an increased focus on fulfilling the soul's purpose or soul's work. The readjustment is not easy work as the hellfires of grief create a very chaotic experience to compound the intense need to reevaluate one's life for its meaning and purpose. The intense necessity to better understand one's soul's needs often require seeking beyond the veil. With the experience of the disembodiment of a loved one, death moves from an abstract concept to an intensely painful reality residing within the heart.

Not all who experience the loss of a loved one become seekers, but for many loss creates the circumstances for a major life adjustment, readjustment, and perhaps transformation. The person may become more heart centered, processing experience more from the heart than the head. The trauma of loss and resulting disorganization and reorganization, often moves the grieving individual to consider matters of the heart as primary. These changes, like the loss itself, may not be a welcome experience. This is an alchemical process that happens outside one's logical rational control just like many of the other elements of loss and grief. With grief work, the breaking of the heart can result in a softer heart and a transformed person.

When writing about these alchemical processes they appear to be orderly and progress in a linear fashion, when in reality the alchemy of grief is the most painful experience with chaos, confusion, and despair prevailing. Once experienced the concepts, images, and processes of alchemy may provide a crude form of guidance to assist in coping with the experience of loss and accompanying grief.

*Dennis William Hauck. **The Emerald Tablet: Alchemy for Personal Transformation.** Penguin, 1999, page 45.

111 Things That Help Grieving: **#108**

Fermentation: Alchemy

The alchemical process of fermentation applied to loss and grief is experienced as the dark night of the soul, which includes the experiences of burning, flooding, separation, and joining of old and new, creating a cauldron of chaos, confusion, and black despair. The initial phase of fermentation is referred to as putrefaction where the chaos of thoughts, feelings, values, hopes, dreams, and trauma are tossed together resulting in the experience of intense heat.

Much of the experience of grief is a private personal matter taking place in the darkness of one's heart of hearts. Some of the grief experience is shared with family and close friends, but much of the work of grieving takes place underground often outside of conscious awareness. The value of the concepts and images of alchemy is not to explain away the experiences, but to accept them as natural consequences of loss and to embrace the experience of the dark night of the soul rather than fight or flee or freeze. The embrace of chaos is much easier said than done. The image is riding a dragon in the dark of the storm, then being swallowed by the dragon while at the same time swallowing the dragon named grief. The experience is one of black despair dropping ever lower into the dragon while the dragon drops ever lower within.

Over time the putrefaction process produces changes in the materials within the caldron as the fermentation process becomes infused with spirit which includes inspirations from the spirit realm. Western alchemists described the beginning of this process as seeing the peacock's tail or the production of the yellow ferment, while Eastern alchemists refer to the golden pill or golden elixir. In the alchemy of grief, the process of fermentation eventually produces the raw materials of transformation. Assisted by a broken heart, and therefore an open heart, one may become more receptive to subtle inspirations, subtle messages, golden dreams, and other assistance from the subtle spirit realm. The alchemical process of fermentation provides the experiences enabling one to transform the black dragon of grief into something else (perhaps the golden rainbow dragon of one's higher self).

The transformation process requires the alchemical operation of distillation to separate, extract, and purify the gold that results from the fermentation process. Repeated distillations are required as measured not in months but years and years.

111 Things That Help Grieving: **#109**

Distillation: Alchemy

"It rises from Earth to Heaven and descends again to Earth thereby combining within Itself the powers of both the Above and Below."
>**The Emerald Tablet**
>translated by Dennis William Hauck*

The alchemical process of distillation involves heating the substance (usually a suspension or compound in liquid), condensing and collecting the vapors that rise, and separating them from the base materials. The process of distillation results in the purified essence being converted (transformed) into vapor and then cooled and condensed into liquid. The distillation of fermented grapes (wine) separates the essence of wine to produce brandy (cognac).

In the process of distillation as applied to the alchemy of grief, the products of earlier processes are collected and transformed by repeated heating and condensing until the essences (physical realm concentrations) are converted into their quintessences. Distillation is an above or higher form of separation that is more subtle, as it is infused with elements of spirit. While the essences may be considered a physical realm concentration, the formation of quintessences includes spirit realm energies.

The process of distillation is a subtle process repeated over and over, involving multiple levels of experience including physical, emotional, psychological, mental, social, soul, and spirit. The alchemical processes of calcination, dissolution, separation, and conjunction are considered the lesser work of purification (the below) while fermentation, distillation, and coagulation are considered the greater work (the above).

In the alchemy of grief, the distillation process provides a brief glimpse of a separate, transpersonal experience of the subtle spirit realm and the dawning awareness of the eternal nature of the energies of life and love. At this stage of my personal distillation process, I am unable to provide more information beyond speculation. If you have been blessed to remember your golden dreams where you have visited the spirit realm and your disembodied loved ones, you have personal experience of the greater work.

The distillation process in the alchemy of grief slowly, with great effort, and considerable pain transforms the ugly reality of the experience of loss of a loved one into the slow dawning awareness, after repeated experiences of the spirit realm, that the disembodied love one has changed forms and can be experienced in a different way. In my experience, this awareness does not remove the intense grief of loss; however, with increased awareness of the subtle spirit realm the energies of eternal love start to balance the experience of loss.

The distillation process in the alchemy of grief is repeated over and over. As noted by Frater

Albertus: "Alchemy is a slow process. It is evolution, the raising of vibrations. It is not a subject that can be mastered by means of the intellectual facilities alone."**

Marie-Louise von Franz in writing about the distillation process states: "That is the *prima materia* which has to be constantly washed and distilled and thus the first activity of the opus (work) is distilling, washing, and cleansing, over and over. Here it says nine times, others say fifteen times, and some say ten years. It is really a very long process and sometimes means endlessly rehearsing the same problem in its different aspects." ***

While much of the alchemy of grief takes place in the dark beyond conscious awareness, experiences of the subtle spirit realm begins a dawning awareness leading to a transformation which offers solace, comfort, and increased potential to part the veil and experience the energies of eternal love.

---

*Dennis William Hauck. **The Emerald Tablet: Alchemy for Personal Transformation**. Penguin, 1999, page 45.

Frater Albertus. **Alchemist's Handbook: Manual for Practical Laboratory Alchemy. Red Wheel/Weiser, 1974, page 28.

***Marie-Louise von Franz. **Alchemy: An Introduction to the Symbolism and the Psychology**. Inner City Books, 1980, pages 221-222.

111 Things That Help Grieving: **#110**

Coagulation: Alchemy

"Thus will you obtain the Glory of the Whole Universe. All Obscurity will be clear to you. This is the greatest Force of all powers, because it overcomes every Subtle Thing and penetrates every Solid Thing."
                        The Emerald Tablet*
                        translated by Dennis William Hauck

The alchemical process of coagulation is beyond my experience; therefore, this thing that helps grieving will be based upon research. The process of coagulation transcends the alchemy of grief as the coagulation is between soul and spirit, transcending the dichotomy of above and below. In psychological terms this reality is briefly experienced in peak experiences and other mystical experiences. The merger of the physical realm with the spirit realm produces what different wisdom traditions refer to as the golden or diamond body. The physical realm self merges with the larger spirit realm SELF to first transcend and then transmute the nature of reality. If you have had the experience of meeting and perhaps merging with your higher SELF, if only for a brief moment or two, you will never forget the experience and be changed since you now have direct experience of the beyond. You will return to ordinary reality, but your experience of your spirit realm home will expand your awareness beyond the confines of ordinary reality. You will not need to believe in your higher SELF, your spirit realm home, and eternal love, you will have experienced the celestial realm and hold the experiences in your heart of hearts.

A book engraving from 1888 illustrates the experience. The wood print, often referred to as the spiritual pilgrim, depicts a young alchemist on the mountain with his head having left the ordinary reality of the physical realm having awakened in the spirit realm. In the print, his head has broken through ordinary reality parting the veil between the below and the above. This print has always held a special fascination for me as it represents, even if briefly, the great work of alchemy: the transformation and eventual transmutation of the individual merged with their higher SELF.

May you remember your experiences of coagulation. Nothing else has the healing power of merging, even if only briefly as in golden dreams, with your higher SELF and meeting your loved ones in their celestial forms. The experience is transformational, as now you know the reality of your spirit realm home. These experiences can be very brief and at least in my experience culminate in returning to the lead body and lead mind of ordinary reality; however, the experience adds to the golden rainbow energy field and raises vibrational levels even if only a little. At this point in my alchemy of grief, it is the best I can do within my limitations. It will have to be enough for now.

*Dennis William Hauck. **The Emerald Tablet Alchemy for Personal Transformation**, Penguin, 1999, page 45.

111 Things That Help Grieving: #111

Transformation/Transmutation: Alchemy

Soon after rediscovering my soulmate in this life time, she gave me what I thought was a heart shaped stone with the saying "grow old along with me the best is yet to be" with a butterfly painted beside the saying. The grow old with me stone, as I referred to the gift, I interpreted as her promise to grow old with me and treasured the gift and even more her promise. After my beloved's disembodiment, I held the grow old with me stone with intense heart breaking despair wondering what had happened to her promise. Holding the grow old with me stone I realized through my tears that the stone was not, after all, a stone but a heart shaped seed. I understood the message that my beloved soulmate intended. She had not promised to grow old but to be along with me as I grow old. The heart shaped seed does not germinate in physical reality, rather requires that I transform my concrete thinking into the higher level spirit realm experience of her transmuted spirit realm form. The grow old with me seed still reminds me of her promise as now I am aware of its subtle spirit realm message. Her promise remains as I now understand the true nature of her promise made so many years ago. She has always been beyond me in so many ways and I work hard to keep up. It has taken over thirty six years for me to truly comprehend and fully appreciate the treasure and promise of the grow old with me seed. I moved the grow old with me seed from its place on the desk to my beloved's shrine where it reminds me of her promise and our eternal love.

Index

(Books listed in **bold**)

	Page
A	
A Shaman's Miraculous Tools	249
A Time To Grieve	213
acupuncture	205
alchemy: concepts & images	255
alchemy of love & loss	260
alchemy: processes & operations	257
animal companions	164
B	
balance, achieving	170
basic bodily functions	198
Being With Dying	223
black bow door decoration	112
black lightning	24
burning incense	95
C	
calcinations (alchemy)	263
ceremonies	77
chakras & subtle energy	28
chakra cords	31
chaos of grief/stages of grief	36
coagulation (alchemy)	279
conjunction (alchemy)	271
compassion	166
complicated grief	56
courage to grieve	161
crying	14
D	
death as advisor/death as companion	52
Dion Fortune's Book of the Dead	226
disbelief	10

disembodied	22
dissolution (alchemy)	266
distillation (alchemy)	276
dream journaling	116

E
elements at the shrine	92
energy healing	200
enough	168
establishing a shrine	90
eyes of love/eyes of loss	154

F
fermentation (alchemy)	274
flowers at the shrine	93
forgiveness	150

G
golden dreams	140
gratitude	209
grief and disease	206
grief counseling	202
Grief Dreams	237
grief journey/healing journey	192
grief memoirs	127
grief work	84
grieving on installment plan	42

H
healing	137
Healing A Spouse's Grieving Heart	245
hellfires of grief	7
holidays are hell	48
honoring last wishes/last requests	68
honoring the dead	64
How To Heal A Grieving Heart	215

I
inspirations	145
I Wasn't Ready To Say Goodbye	241

J
journaling 114
Journey of Souls 243

K
kindness 158

L
life review 74
life transforming moments 26
lighting candles 94

M
maintaining traditions 82
making room 148
massage therapy 204
meditation to ease grief (CD) 132
memorials 99
memories/reminiscences 87
messages 142
moratorium on holidays/celebrations 80
music 98

N
naming grief 70

O
On Dreams and Death 233
One Spirit Medicine 250
On Grief and Grieving 229

P
photographs 96
planting a tree 104
poems/poetry 119
possession in great measure 156
projects 134

Q
quintessence, sharing (alchemy) 172

R

raw	12
reading bereavement books	124
reality of my experience	40
regrets and remorse	50
residual energy	190

S

sadness and depression	59
separation (alchemy)	269
Shaman, Healer, Sage	247
sharing stories	109
sick room things, removing	108
soft heart, open heart, broken heart	20
soror mystica (alchemy)	182
soulmates guardian angels	180
soulmatespiritmates	175
spirit warrior	195
support of family and friends	188
Swallowed By A Snake	221

T

talking with my spirit companion	186
The Emerald Tablet	251
The Five Ways We Grieve	239
The Way Men Heal	219
Transcending Loss	217
transformation/transmutation (alchemy)	281
triggers	44

U

using disembodied's things	106

W

wearing black	102
widower/widow	54
within my limitations	152
woundedness	17

Books (also listed in alpha index in bold):

A Time To Grieve	213
How To Heal A Grieving Heart	215
Transcending Loss	217
The Way Men Heal	219
Swallowed By A Snake	221
Being With Dying	223
Gates of Death/Book of the Dead	226
On Grief and Grieving	229
On Dreams and Death	233
Grief Dreams	237
Five Ways We Grieve	239
I Wasn't Ready To Say Goodbye	241
Journey of Souls	243
Healing A Spouse's Grieving Heart	245
Shaman, Healer, Sage	247
A Shaman's Miraculous Tools	249
One Spirit Medicine	250
The Emerald Tablet	251

Alchemy of the Heart (also listed in alpha index):

Alchemy: Concepts and Images	255
Alchemy: Processes and Operations	257
Alchemy of Love/Alchemy of Loss	260
Calcination (fire)	263
Dissolution (water)	266
Separation (air)	269
Conjunction (earth)	271
Fermentation	274
Distillation	276
Coagulation	279
Transformation/Transmutation	281
Quintessence, sharing	172
Soror Mystica	182

Acknowledgements

Celestial Helpers-Healers:
Carol Susan, Carlos Eldon, and others

Embodied Helpers-Healers:
Carol Susan, Carlos Eldon, Taryne Jade, Denise Conner, Maya and Merlin, Lauren, Deb Cannon, Dede Dancing, Alice Claussen, Johanna Moorman, Carol Pollock, Nancy Powell, Julia Buchkina, and others

Taylor DeVaney Wong Family Support:
Especially Taryne Jade, Bob, Martha, Itzel, Manuella, Mater, Doris, Diana, Carmen, Alfonso, Fanny and Tommy, Ceci, Chicho, and others

Special thanks to Denise E. Conner who graciously read the first draft of **111 Things That Help Grieving** and made excellent suggestions to improve clarity and readability. The content and any remaining errors are solely my responsibility.

Copyright Acknowledgement/ Permissions

I wish to provide copyright acknowledgement and thank the publishers for permission to reprint excerpts from the following (in order of first appearance):

Section 1: Experience of Grief: Words/Concepts/Images

from **Alchemy: An Introduction to the Symbolism and the Psychology** by Marie-Louise von Franz, ©1980 by Marie-Louise von Franz, published by Inner City Books.

from **A Grief Observed** by C.S. Lewis, ©1961 under the pseudonym N. W. Clerk, restored 1996 to C. S. Lewis Pte. Ltd., published by Harper Collins.

from **Light Emerging: The Journey of Personal Healing** by Barbara A. Brennan, ©1993 by Barbara A. Brennan, published by Bantam Books/Random House.

from **Hands of Light: A Guide to Healing Through the Human Energy Field** by Barbara A. Brennan, ©1987 by Barbara A. Brennan, published by Bantam Books/Random House.

from **On Grief and Grieving: Finding the Meaning of Grief Through the Five Stages of Loss** by Elisabeth Kubler-Ross and David Kessler, ©2005 by Elisabeth Kubler-Ross Family Limited Partnership and David Kessler Inc., published by Scribner/SimonSchuster.

from **A Meditation To Ease Grief** (CD) by Belleruth Naparstek, ©1992 by Belleruth Naparstek, published by Health Journeys.

from **Being with Dying: Cultivating Compassion and Fearlessness in the Presence of Death** by Joan Halifax, ©2008 by Joan Halifax, published by Shambhala.

from **The Importance of Living** by Lin Yutang, ©1995 by Lin Tai-yi and Hsiang Ju Lin, published by Harper.

from **DSM-5 Fact Sheet: Major Depressive Disorder and the "Bereavement Exclusion,"** by the American Psychiatric Association, ©2013 by American Psychiatric Association, published by the American Psychiatric Association.

Section 2: Activities/Actions/Doings

from **The Red Book: Liber Novus: A Reader's Edition** by C.G. Jung, ©2009 by The Foundation of the Works of C. G. Jung, published by W. W. Norton.

from **Soul Mates: Honoring the Mysteries of Love and Relationship** by Thomas Moore, ©1994 by Thomas Moore, published by Harper Collins.

from **Dion Fortune's Book of the Dead** by Dion Fortune , ©2000 by the Society of Inner Light, London, published by Weiser Books, (first published as **Through the Gates of Death** in 1930).

from **On Dreams & Death** by Marie-Louise von Franz, ©1994 by Kosel-Verlag Gmblt & Co., translation © 1986 by Shambhala, published by Shambhala.

from **The Wisdom of Your Dreams: Using Dreams To Tap Into Your Unconscious and Transform Your Life** by Jeremy Taylor, ©2009 by Jeremy Taylor, published by Jeremy P. Tarcher/Penguin.

from **Dark Nights of the Soul: A Guide To Finding Your Way Through Life's Ordeals** by Thomas Moore, ©2004 by Thomas Moore, published by Penguin.

from **Poetic Medicine: The Healing Act of Poem Making** by John Fox, ©1997 by John Fox, published by Jeremy P. Tarcher/Putnam

from "To Have Loved and Lost" by Meghan O'Rourke, from **The New York Times Book Review**, April 26, 2015, page 16, ©The New York Times, published by The New York Times.

from **The Best Day The Worst Day: Life With Jane Kenyon,** by Donald Hall, ©2005 by Donald Hall, published by Houghton Mifflin.

Section 3: Healing

from **Chicken Soup for the Grieving Soul: Stories About Life, Death and Overcoming the Loss of a Loved One** by Jack Canfried and Mark Victor Hansen, ©2012 by Chicken Soup for the Soul Publishing, **"I Wish You Enough"** by Bob Perks, ©2001 by Bob Perks, published by Chicken Soup for the Soul Publishing.

from **Mysteruim Coniunctionis, Collected Works, Volume 14** by C. G. Jung, ©1963 by Bollingen Foundation, published by Princeton University Press.

from **A Commentary on the Mutus Liber: Magnum Opus Hermetic Sourceworks #11** by Adam McLean, ©1991 by Adam McLean, published by Phanes Press.

from **Shambhala: The Sacred Path of the Warrior** by Chogyam Trungpa, ©1984 by Diana J. Mukpo, published by Shambhala.

Section 4: Book Resources

from **Language of the Night: Essays on Fantasy and Science Fiction** by Ursula K. Le Guin, ©1979 by Ursula K. Le Guin, published in revised edition 1992 by HarperCollins.

from **A Time To Grieve: Meditations for Healing After the Death of a Loved One** by Carol Staudacher, ©1994 by Carol Staudacher, published by Harper Collins.

from **How To Heal A Grieving Heart** by Doreen Virtue and James Van Praagh, ©2013 by Doreen Virtue and James Van Praagh, published by Hay House.

from **Healing with the Angels: How the Angels Can Assist You in Every Area of Your Life** by Doreen Virtue, ©1999 by Doreen Virtue, published by Hay House.

from **Growing Up In Heaven: The Eternal Connection Between Parent and Child** by James Van Praagh, ©2011 by James Van Praagh, published by Harper Collins.

from **Transcending Loss: Understanding the Lifelong Impact of Grief and How to Make It Meaningful** by Ashley Davis Bush, ©1997 by Ashley D. Prend, published by Berkley Books/Penguin.

from **The Way Men Heal** by Tom Golden, ©2013 by Golden Healing Publishing, published by Golden Healing Publishing.

from **Swallowed by a Snake: The Gift of the Masculine Side of Healing** by Tom Golden, ©2000 by Golden Healing Publishing, published by Golden Healing Publishing.

from **Grief Dreams: How They Help Heal Us After the Death of a Loved One** by T. J. Wray and Ann Back Price, ©2005 by T. J. Wray and Ann Back Price, published by Jossey-Bass.

from **The Five Ways We Grieve: Finding Your Personal Path to Healing after the Loss of a Loved One** by Susan A. Berger, ©2009 by Susan A. Berger, published by Trumpeter Books/Shambhala.

from **I Wasn't Ready To Say Goodbye: Surviving, Coping, and Healing After the Sudden Death of a Loved One** by Brook Noel and Pamela D. Blair, ©2008 by Brook Noel and Pamela D. Blair, published by Sourcebooks.

from **Healing A Spouse's Grieving Heart: 100 Practical Ideas After Your Husband or Wife Dies: Compassionate Advice and Simple Activities for Widows and Widowers**, by Alan D. Wolfelt, ©2003 by Alan D. Wolfelt, published by Companion Press.

from **Shaman, Healer, Sage: How To Heal Yourself and Others with the Energy Medicine of the Americas** by Alberto Villoldo, ©2000 by Alberto Villoldo, published by Random House.

Section 5: Alchemy of the Heart

from **Psychology and Alchemy, Collected Works, Volume 12, Second Edition** by C. G. Jung, ©1953 by Bollingen Foundation, published by Princeton University Press.

from **The Emerald Tablet: Alchemy for Personal Transformation** by Dennis William Hauck, ©1999 by Dennis William Hauck, published by Penguin.

from **Alchemist's Handbook: Manual for Practical Laboratory Alchemy** by Frater Albertus, ©1974 by the estate of Frater Albertus, published by Red Wheel/Weiser.

Author

C. Eldon Taylor is a psychotherapist licensed as a Licensed Professional Counselor (LPC-Virginia), Licensed Mental Health Counselor (LMHC-Florida), and National Certified Counselor. None of which was much help when it became his turn to experience the hellfires of grief and black nights of the soul after the disembodiment of his beloved Carol Susan.

Contact Information:
celdontaylor@gmail.com

Other Works by the Author

On November 22, 2011, I was inspired to start keeping a journal. I write in the journal every day, usually late at night. In October 2012, I was inspired to condense my experiences recorded in the journals into free form poems.

Hellfires of Grief: Love Poems was published in May of 2013. **Hellfires I** (as I refer to the book) consists of 222 poems providing an intimate description of the hellfires of grief and black nights of the soul I experienced during the first eighteen months of my bereavement. The poems were written to translate my tears of grief into words as part of my healing journey. The poems were published to share my experience and provide a crude map for others experiencing their own versions of the hellfires of grief.

Golden Dreams: Companion to Hellfires of Grief: Love Poems was published in November of 2013. **Golden Dreams I** is a collection of 111 poems describing the golden dreams shared with my disembodied beloved during the first eighteen months of my bereavement. **Golden Dreams I** provides my dreamtime experiences as a counterpoint to my daytime experiences described in **Hellfires I**. The 111 poems in **Golden Dreams I** are condensed from dream journals starting with the first golden dream of January 5, 2012 and continuing to the 111th golden dream of October 9, 2013. Not all of the dreams are golden as some do not include my disembodied beloved's beautiful radiant golden aura. The overall energy of **Golden Dreams I** is golden providing a healing counterpart to the intense darkness of **Hellfires I**. The poems of **Hellfires I** are lit by the black fires of the hell of loss and grief while **Golden Dreams I** is illuminated by the celestial golden light of love. Shared golden dreams start the process of healing and provide a glimpse into the realm of spirit. Shared golden dreams spill into waking time slowly transforming the grief dragon described in **Hellfires I**. Golden dreams have provided the most powerful healing experience of my bereavement.

Taken together, **Hellfires I** and **Golden Dreams I** are a total of 333 free form poems covering the first eighteen months after the disembodiment of my soulmate. The two books provide an unusual form of grief memoir, nearly written in real time, of the first year and one half.

Hellfires of Grief II: More Love Poems was published in November 2014. **Hellfires II** is a collection of 222 poems written during the second eighteen months of my bereavement. Together **Hellfires I** and **Hellfires II** cover the first three years of my experiences of loss, grief, despair, and the slow transformation from seeing only with eyes of loss to also seeing with eyes of love. The combined 444 poems (750 pages) summarize my waking experience.

Golden Dreams II is currently in process. The delay is in part due to only including golden dreams, as well as my well developed dream forgetting skills. When completed, perhaps later in 2016, **Golden Dreams II** will begin with dreams from October of 2013 and present 111 golden dreams as free form poems. Together **Golden Dreams I** and **Golden Dreams II** will summarize my nighttime dreaming experiences for the first five years of bereavement in 222 dream poems. The healing power of golden dreams cannot be described with words. When I am tempted to complain about the Goddess of Dreams not assisting me in remembering more golden dreams, I need only to read from the collection of golden dreams to experience their healing energy and renew my appreciation and gratitude for remembering so many visits to the spirit realm.

Heartfires of Love is another work in progress and will consist of an additional 222 poems which start at the end of the third year of bereavement and continue until the 222nd poem has been completed. Currently at about twenty-five percent completed, **Heartfires of Love** will be completed within the next several years.

The poems have provided much of the raw material that has been distilled and condensed into **111 Things That Help Grieving: Alchemy of the Heart: Love Loss Grief Transformation Eternal Love.**

www.ingramcontent.com/pod-product-compliance
Lightning Source LLC
LaVergne TN
LVHW011910080426
835508LV00007BA/324